Collins

11+
Maths

Complete Revision, Practice & Assessment

For the CEM test

11+ Tests and Maths

CEM (The Centre for Evaluation and Monitoring) is one of the two major bodies responsible for setting 11+ tests.

The CEM exam usually consists of two papers and in each paper pupils are tested on their skills in verbal, non-verbal and numerical reasoning. Exams are separated into short, timed sections delivered by audio instructions.

It appears the content required for CEM exams changes from year to year, and the level at which pupils are tested ranges from county to county. Before sitting the exam, your child should be well prepared, with solid foundations built in the three core skills.

It is important to provide maths practice as the 11+ exam may test reasoning and problem-solving skills that are slightly more advanced than those on the national curriculum for your child's age.

About this Book

This book is split into three sections to help children to prepare for the numerical reasoning components of the CEM test. Features of each section include:

Revision

- Easy-to-digest revision notes for each topic.
- Develops the skills needed to answer test questions.
- 'Remember' boxes to emphasise key points and provide tips.
- Quick Tests to check understanding of a topic before moving on.

Practice

- Topic-based questions to practise the necessary skills.
- Increases familiarity with the questions expected in the test.
- Tests are timed to develop the ability to work at speed.

Assessment

- Three assessment papers offer multiple opportunities to have a go at a test and gradually improve performance.
- Familiarises your child with the potential format of the papers.
- Enables your child to practise working at speed and with accuracy.

Answers and explanations are provided at the back of the book to help you mark your child's answers and support their preparation.

Progress charts are also included for recording scores on the practice tests and assessment papers.

ebook

To access the ebook visit collins.co.uk/ebooks and follow the step-by-step instructions.

The Assessment Papers

Spend some time talking with your child so that they understand the purpose of the assessment papers and how doing them will help them to prepare for the actual exam.

Agree with your child a good time to take the assessment papers. This should be when they are fresh and alert. You also need to find a good place to work, a place that is comfortable and free from distractions. Being able to see a clock is helpful as they learn how to pace themselves.

Explain how they may find some parts easy and others more challenging, but that they need to have a go at every question. If they 'get stuck' on a question, they should just mark it with an asterisk and carry on. At the end of the section, they may have time to go back and try again.

As in the actual test, the answers to the assessment papers should not be written on the question booklet. They should be marked on the separate answer sheet (as in the real test a computer will be used in the marking process). Answers should be carefully marked in pencil with a straight line on the answer sheet.

Answer sheets for the practice tests and the assessment papers can be found on pages 155–168. Further copies of these answer sheets can be downloaded from **collins.co.uk/11plus**.

Question Types and Time Allocation

In the actual test, your child is likely to be expected to answer questions presented in different styles, including multiple choice, cloze and marking-the-digits. These are explained in greater detail on page 5 and practice for these different question formats is provided throughout this book.

The time allowed is given on the introductory pages for each part of the assessment papers. These timings are based on the challenging time allocations that would be expected in the actual 11+ exam. CEM tests are designed to be time pressured and you don't necessarily need to complete all the questions to pass or do well.

If your child has not finished after the allocated time, ask them to draw a line to indicate where they are on the test at that time, and allow them to finish. This allows them to practise every question type, as well as allowing you to get a score showing how many were correctly answered in the time available. It will also help you and your child to think about ways to increase speed of working if this is an area that your child finds difficult. If your child completes a section in less than the allocated minutes, encourage them to go through and check their answers carefully.

Marking

Award one mark for each correct answer. Half marks are not allowed. No marks are deducted for wrong answers.

If scores are low, look at the paper and identify which question types seem to be harder for your child. Then spend some time going over them together. If your child is very accurate and gets correct answers, but works too slowly, try getting them to do one of the tests with time targets going through. If you are helpful and look for ways to help your child, they will grow in confidence and feel well prepared when they take the actual exam.

Please note: The score achieved on these papers is no guarantee that your child will achieve a score of the same standard on the formal tests.

Collins is not associated with CEM in any way. This book does not contain any official questions and it is not endorsed by CEM.

Our question types are based on those set by CEM, but we cannot guarantee that your child's actual 11+ exam will contain the same question types or format as this book.

Contents & Acknowledgements

Revision

Practice

Assessment

Answers

Acknowledgements

The authors and publisher are grateful to the copyright holders for permission to use quoted materials and images.

All images are © Shutterstock.com and © HarperCollinsPublishers Ltd

Every effort has been made to trace copyright holders and obtain their permission for the use of copyright material. The authors and publisher will gladly receive information enabling them to rectify any error or omission in subsequent editions. All facts are correct at time of going to press.

Published by Collins
An imprint of HarperCollinsPublishers
1 London Bridge Street
London SE1 9GF

ISBN: 978-0-00-839889-7

First published 2020

10 9 8 7 6 5 4 3 2 1

© HarperCollinsPublishers Ltd. 2020

British Library Cataloguing in Publication Data.

A CIP record of this book is available from the British Library.

Publishers: Clare Souza and Katie Sergeant
Contributing authors: Faisal Nasim, Leisa Bovey, Peter Derych, Phil Duxbury, Val Mitchell, Sally Moon, Donna Hanley, Rosie Benton, Rob Kearsley-Bullen and Howard Macmillan
Project Development and Management: Rebecca Skinner and Richard Toms
Cover Design: Kevin Robbins and Sarah Duxbury
Inside Concept Design: Ian Wrigley
Page Layout: Jouve India Private Limited
Production: Karen Nulty
Printed by CPI Group (UK) Ltd, Croydon CR0 4YY

MIX
Paper from responsible sources
FSC™ C007454
www.fsc.org

This book is produced from independently certified FSC™ paper to ensure responsible forest management.

For more information visit: **www.harpercollins.co.uk/green**

Introduction to Question Formats

You should be able to:

- answer multiple-choice questions, including cloze questions
- answer questions by marking the correct digits.

Test Format and Question Types

- In the actual test, you are likely to have to work through question booklets which include two or more maths sections.
- You will give your answers on a separate answer sheet by carefully marking a straight line with a pencil through your chosen option.
- You need to be prepared to answer questions in the formats described below and this book provides opportunities to practise these different styles.

Multiple Choice

- Most of the questions in the test are likely to be multiple choice.
- Some questions may simply offer five answer options, labelled **A, B, C, D** and **E**, for you to choose from.
- Other sections may offer a greater range of answer options (e.g. **A, B, C, D, E, F, G, H, I** and **J**) and you will have to choose answers to a group of questions from this set of options.
- You will need to mark the letter for your chosen answer option in the correct place on the answer sheet.

Cloze

- In cloze questions, you could be presented with some information and then asked to complete sentences that have gaps for you to fill in.
- You could be asked to select your answers from a set of multiple-choice options, marking the letter for your chosen answer on the answer sheet.

Mark the Digits

- For other questions, you may be asked to mark the numerical digits of the answer on the sheet.
- The answer sheet will have two columns of digits from 0 to 9, so for an answer with two digits (e.g. '16') you would mark '1' in the first column and '6' in the second column.
- For questions with a one-digit answer (e.g. 'What is 15 – 10?'), you still need to complete both columns by marking '0' in the first column and, in this case, '5' in the second column.

Remember

You will be allowed to use an HB pencil, a rubber and a pencil in the test. However, you will **not** be allowed to use a ruler, a protractor or a calculator.

Remember

The actual test will include example questions and answers to help to show you what to do.

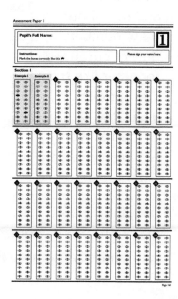

Number and Place Value

You should be able to:

- read, write and interpret numbers expressed as numerals and in words
- order positive and negative numbers
- round a number to the nearest ten, hundred or thousand
- solve problems using numerical reasoning.

Place Value and Reading and Writing Numbers

- Place value means that with only 10 symbols (0, 1, 2, 3, 4, 5, 6, 7, 8, 9) you can write any number of any size.
- The table shows some positions and their place values:

9	6	5	3	8	1	4	.	7	2
MILLIONS	HUNDRED THOUSANDS	TEN THOUSANDS	THOUSANDS	HUNDREDS	TENS	ONES (UNITS)	DECIMAL POINT	TENTHS	HUNDREDTHS

> **Remember**
>
> The position of each digit in a number is related to its magnitude (i.e. its size).

- If asked how many thousands there are in a number, look at the thousands column and read the numeral in that position. In the number 9,653,814.72 there are three thousands.

Example

How many hundreds are there in the number 27,978?

27,978

There are **9** hundreds.

- To read, write and talk about these numbers they get grouped together like this:
- The number 9,653,814.72 written as words

9	6	5 3	8	1 4	.	7	2
Million	Hundred and	Thousand	Hundred and		Point		

is: nine million, six hundred and fifty-three thousand, eight hundred and fourteen point seven two.

> **Remember**
>
> Be careful when there are places that contain zeros. The number three thousand and ninety-two has no hundreds; it is the same as 'three thousand, no hundreds and ninety-two'. In numerals that is 3,092.

Example

What is 403,055 in words?

Four hundred and three thousand and fifty-five

Ordering Whole Numbers

- Ordering numbers is about place value. Check whether you are ordering largest to smallest, or smallest to largest.
- Write the numbers in columns containing thousands, hundreds, tens and ones.

Example

Order these numbers from smallest to largest:

91 996 936 6 1 19 29 0 9,360 963

For ordering whole numbers, group the numbers depending on how many digits they have, then order them within each column:

6	91	996	9,360
1	29	963	
0	19	936	

The correct order of the numbers, smallest to largest, is:

0 1 6 19 29 91 936 963 996 9,360

> **Remember**
>
> When ordering negative numbers, the process is reversed, i.e. two-digit numbers are smaller than one-digit numbers. For example, −60 is less than −5.

Number Lines

- Number lines help you to think about the relative positions of numbers.
- Some number lines include negative numbers. The numbers become more negative as they move left (or down). You may need to interpret these numbers in a given context.
- When reading a number line:
  - make sure you check what the labelled numbers go up in
  - look at how the gaps between the numbers are divided up and check the sub-divisions make sense.

> **Remember**
>
> Examples of number lines used in real life are the measurements along the edge of a ruler or the scale on a thermometer.

Example

Read the points labelled A, B and C on the number line below.

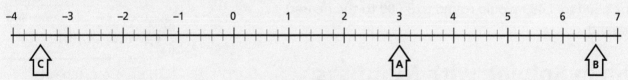

The point A is at a labelled point so can be read straight off. **A = 3**

The point B is on one of the sub-divisions. The gap between labelled points is 1. There are five steps (sub-divisions) between each labelled point so the smaller divisions are steps of 1 ÷ 5 = 0.2. You can check this by writing in the steps.

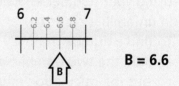

B = 6.6

The point C sits in the middle of two sub-divisions. What number is halfway between −3.4 and −3.6?

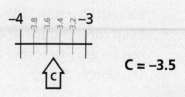

C = −3.5

- You can use number lines to count on or back from a given number too.

Example

This is a picture of the thermometer in Sarah's greenhouse.

The greenhouse is 7.5°C warmer than outside.

What is the temperature outside?

Each small sub-division is 2.5°C.

So the reading on this thermometer is –2.5°C.

7.5°C colder would be **–10°C**.

Rounding Whole Numbers

- Not all rounding questions use the word 'rounding'. Other words used include 'sensible', and 'roughly'.
- Before you begin, check which place value you are rounding to: tens, hundreds or thousands.
- When rounding to tens, look at the digit in the ones (units) column: digits 1 to 4 round to the ten below; digits 5 to 9 round to the ten above.

All round down to 20 to the nearest ten.   All round up to 30 to the nearest ten.

20 21 22 23 24 25 26 27 28 29 30

- When rounding to hundreds, look at the digit in the tens column and apply the same rule. So, for example, all numbers from 150 to 249 would round to 200 to the nearest hundred.
- When rounding to thousands, look at the digit in the hundreds column and apply the same rule. So, for example, all numbers from 2,500 to 3,499 would round to 3,000 to the nearest thousand.

> **Remember**

If a number is exactly halfway between two tens, two hundreds or two thousands, the rule is **round up**.

Problem Solving with Numbers

- Using your number knowledge, it is possible to solve questions in unfamiliar contexts.
- To find a number halfway between two given numbers:
  - Add the two numbers together and divide by 2; this is quick but the calculation might be complicated.
  - Count, on a number line, back from one number and forward from the other until you meet in the middle – keep careful track of doing the same from both sides as it can be easy to forget and move further from one side than the other.

> **Remember**

There are often lots of ways to come up with solutions to mathematical questions. Use the way that makes sense to you and think about how you could explain your method to someone else.

- Find how big the gap is between the two numbers (take the smaller one away from the larger), halve the answer, then add it onto the smaller number (or take it away from the larger number).

Example

What number is halfway between 17 and 35?

$17 + 35 = 52$ $\frac{52}{2} = 26$	~~17~~, ~~18~~, ~~19~~, ~~20~~, ~~21~~, ~~22~~, ~~23~~, ~~24~~, 25, ~~26~~, ~~27~~, ~~28~~, ~~29~~, ~~30~~, ~~31~~, ~~32~~, ~~33~~, ~~34~~, ~~35~~ Ensure that an equal number of values are crossed out on each side.	$35 - 17 = 18$ $\frac{18}{2} = 9$ $17 + 9 = \mathbf{26}$

- For problem-solving questions, often the best approach is to try something, test it out and see if it helps to find a way towards a solution. If a method is taking a long time, then look for any patterns or shortcuts that you could use.

Example

Arenya is playing a game where she spins a spinner to get a starting number. She then counts up by 3, then 7, then 3, then 7, and so on. She wins the game if she gets to say the number 37. Which number(s) on the spinner must Arenya get on the spinner in order to win?

Since 3 and 7 are number bonds to 10 (i.e. 3 + 7 = 10), the units as she counts will repeat so it is possible to see whether a starting point will give a result of 37 without needing to do the counting beyond 37 for each number.

Starting at 1, 4, 11, 14, ... this will not give 37 as it will always have a final digit of 1 or 4.

2, 5, 12, 15, ... 3, 6, 13, 16, ...

4, 7, 14, 17, ... starting on 4 will get to 37.

5, 8, 15, 18, ... 6, 9, 16, 19, ...

4 is the only number that will get her to 37.

> **Quick Test**

1. Write the number ten thousand and sixty-five in numerals.
2. Write the number 370,806 in words.
3. The price of a house is £224,945. What is this rounded to:
   a) the nearest ten?   b) the nearest thousand?
   c) the nearest hundred thousand?
4. Which of these cities is the coldest?
   A Birmingham 0°C   B Exeter 8°C   C Leeds –3°C
   D London 5°C   E Newcastle –8°C
5. These six-digit numbers are listed in order but some of the digits have been replaced by boxes. Fill in the missing digits.
   342,95☐
   342,☐51
   ☐49,808
   3☐9,806
   359,☐45

Calculations

You should be able to:

- find an efficient method to add, subtract, multiply and divide numbers
- solve complex multiplications and divisions
- choose the correct operation to solve and follow the BIDMAS rule
- use rounding to predict answers and check for accuracy.

Mental Strategies

Addition and Subtraction Shortcuts

- Although you can always use the column method for additions and subtractions, many questions can be solved by using number bond facts you already know.
- Look for number bonds within lists to speed up addition.

> **Example**
> To add up this list, first identify pairs that you can add easily, then complete the final addition:
> | 109 | 4 | 1 | 91 | 15 |
> |---|---|---|---|---|
>
> 109 + 91 = 200   4 + 1 = 5, then 5 + 15 = 20
> 200 + 20 = **220**

- When subtracting, move the 'gap' between numbers to speed up the calculation. Add an equal value to each number to simplify the calculation. Here the value added is 2:
  $$98 - 72 = \longrightarrow 100 - 74 =$$
- To add or subtract a number, round the 'almost multiple' up or down, calculate and adjust.

> **Example**
> 307 + 199 = ?
>
> 307 + 200 = 507   507 − 1 = **506**

> **Example**
> 307 − 199 = ?
>
> 307 − 200 = 107   107 + 1 = **108**

- When working with positive and negative numbers, it helps to visualise a number line. Moving from left to right along the number line shown here represents addition; working from right to left indicates subtraction.

> **Remember**
>
> Moving the 'gap' is a method that only works with subtraction.

> **Remember**
>
> Subtracting a negative number means that you add it. For example:
> $$3 - (-7) = 10$$

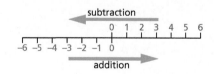

Example

−3 + 4 = ?

Begin at −3 on the number line. Move four numbers to the right to find the answer.

−3 + 4 = **+1**

Example

−3 − 2 = ?

Begin at −3 on the number line. Move two numbers to the left to find the answer.

−3 − 2 = **−5**

Remember

Use inverse operations to check that your answer is correct.

For example, 2,456 + 172 = 2,628, so that means 2,628 − 172 = 2,456.

- When carrying out calculations, you can use partitioning to break down numbers into easier-to-use values, for example thinking of 837 as 800 + 30 + 7.

Example

536 + 628 = ?

Partition both numbers:

536	=	500	+	30	+	6		
628	=	600	+	20	+	8		
Total	=	1,100	+	50	+	14	=	**1,164**

Remember

There are lots of different ways to approach addition and subtraction, which means there is always a way to double check an answer by using a second method.

Multiplication and Division Shortcuts

- Many multiplication and division questions can be solved by using already-known number bond facts.
- Use multiplication tables that you know and look for ways to partition numbers.

Example

17 × 5 = ?

17 × 5 can be split into: 10 × 5 = 50   7 × 5 = 35

Then add the numbers back together:

$$17 \times 5 \begin{array}{c} \nearrow 10 \times 5 = 50 \searrow \\ \\ \searrow 7 \times 5 = 35 \nearrow \end{array} = \textbf{85}$$

- To multiply and divide by 10, 100 and 1,000: move digits to the left when multiplying, and to the right when dividing.
- When dividing, you may have to cross the decimal point.

Example

25 × 10 = 250	25 ÷ 100 = 0.25
25 × 100 = 2,500	250 ÷ 10 = 25
25 × 1,000 = 25,000	2,500 ÷ 100 = 25

- When multiplying by the numbers 9, 99 and 999:
  Round the 9, 99 or 999 to 10, 100 or 1,000 and adjust by subtraction.

Example

$56 \times 9 = ?$

$56 \times 9 = (56 \times 10) - 56$

$56 \times 10 = 560$ $560 - 56 = \mathbf{504}$

- Your knowledge of doubling and halving numbers can also help solve some problems.
- To multiply by 4, double the number twice.

Example

$22 \times 4 = ?$

$22 \times 2 = 44$ and $44 \times 2 = \mathbf{88}$

- To divide by 4, halve the number twice.

Example

$248 \div 4 = ?$

$248 \div 2 = 124$ and $124 \div 2 = \mathbf{62}$

Formal Written Methods

Multiplication

- There are two common methods for solving multiplications:

Column method

$$
\begin{array}{r}
3\ 6\ 2 \\
\times\quad 4\ 3 \\
\hline
1\ 0{,}8\ 6 \quad (362 \times 3) \\
1\ 4{,}4\ 8\ 0 \quad (362 \times 40) \\
\hline
1\ 5\ 5{,}6\ 6 \\
\end{array}
$$

Grid method

×	300	60	2
40	12,000	2,400	80
3	900	180	6

12,900 2,580   86

12,900 + 2,580 + 86 = 15,566

← You must partition the numbers correctly, e.g. $362 = 300 + 60 + 2$

Division

- Use a formal method to solve more complex division questions:

$$
\begin{array}{r}
1\ 2\ 3\ 0 \\
8\overline{)9\ ^18\ ^24\ 0}
\end{array}
$$

- Sometimes a number will divide exactly, leaving a whole number answer; sometimes a division calculation will leave a remainder.
- Division calculations can be thought of as sharing. If you imagine sharing a bag of 19 marbles between a group of five friends, each time round everyone is given a marble. After three rounds, everyone has three marbles but now there are only four marbles left. These four marbles can't be shared fairly between the five friends. The four marbles are the remainder (what is left over when everything that could be divided up in whole parts has been).
- Sometimes it is more appropriate to round the remainder up or down.

> **Remember**
>
> Clue words can suggest the question is about multiplication or division.
>
> Common words for multiplication are: 'altogether', 'total', 'product', 'times' and 'lots of'.
>
> Clue words for division include: 'share', 'remainder', 'left over' and 'quotient'.

Example

Charlie has 57 marbles and wants to share them evenly between his eight friends. How many marbles will each person get and will there be any left over?

$57 \div 8$

$56 = 7 \times 8, 57 - 56 = 1$

$$57 \div 8 = 7 \ remainder \ 1$$

Each person will get **7 marbles** and there will be **1 left over**.

Example

A school has 353 students in a year group. The students must be split into classes of 30. How many classes will there be in this year group?

$353 \div 30$

$300 \div 30 = 10, 30 \div 30 = 1,$

$330 \div 30 = 11$

$353 \div 30 = 11$ remainder 23

There would need to be **12 classes** as there are more than 330 students (which would be 11 classes) and the 23 remaining students need to be included in a class.

Carrying Out the Correct Operations

- Some questions will involve more than one operation and you will need to identify what these are.

Example

Anwar had 385 CDs. He put them into boxes that held 30 each. How many full boxes did he have?

The question could be solved by repeated subtraction or simple division.

$385 - (10 \times 30) = 85$ and $85 - (2 \times 30) = 25$

So there are **12 full boxes** (with 25 CDs left over).

BIDMAS

- BIDMAS is an easy way to remember the order in which operations should be completed:
  Brackets first... then **I**ndices (powers), then **D**ivision and **M**ultiplication, then **A**ddition and **S**ubtraction
- When there are brackets, you must do the calculation within the brackets first otherwise the answer may be incorrect. So $(6 + 3) \times 3 = 27$.
- Without the brackets, the multiplication must be done first, so $6 + 3 \times 3 = 15$.

Remember

Use inverse operations to check that your answer is correct. For example, $17 \times 5 = 85$, so that means $85 \div 5 = 17$.

Remember

The order in which you perform a calculation can affect the answer.

1. In a traffic survey over three days, Samantha observed 180 vehicles in total. She recorded 45 cars on the first day and 40 on the second day. She also saw 61 vans and lorries over the three days. How many cars did she see on the third day?
2. Callum's mobile phone came with 200 free texts. He has replied to 67 texts sent by friends and has sent 49 of his own. How many of his free texts are left?
3. Sophie didn't eat chocolate for 308 days. How many weeks was this?
4. A tray of Baxwell soup holds 12 cans. Jez stacks 252 trays on to the shelves in the supermarket. How many cans are there altogether?
5. Insert brackets in this calculation to make it correct: $76 - 48 \div 12 \div 3 = 7$

Estimating and Checking

- Rounding helps you to roughly predict an answer or to check if a calculation is sensible.

Example

$2,367 + 3,945 + 4,210 = ?$

Rounding to the nearest thousand, this becomes:

$2,000 + 4,000 + 4,000 =$

The answer should be roughly 10,000.

- When you are estimating answers involving large numbers, look for numbers that can be rounded up or down.

Example

$24 \times 693 + 76 \times 591 = ?$

A 6,200   B 61,548   C 69,540   D 32,560   E 58,623,241

The numbers can be rounded to: $20 \times 700 + 80 \times 600 =$

Remembering BIDMAS, $14,000 + 48,000 = 62,000$

Choose the answer closest to the estimate; the answer is **B**.

Factors and Multiples

- **Factors** are all the values that a number can be **divided** by exactly without leaving a remainder. Factors occur in pairs.

Example

To work out the factors of 12: 1×12 2×6 3×4

So the factors of 12 are: 1, 2, 3, 4, 6 and 12

- When finding the factors of a square number, one pair will be the same value multiplied by itself.

Example

To work out the factors of 16: 1×16 2×8 (4×4)

You only write each factor once: 1, 2, 4, 8, 16

- **Prime numbers** only have two factors: 1 and the number itself.

Remember

If the question involves making something smaller, this indicates subtraction or division.

If the question involves making something bigger, this indicates addition or multiplication.

Remember

Numbers that are not prime and are greater than 1 are called **composite numbers**.

- **Multiples** of a number are what you get when you multiply that number by different whole numbers, so the answers are in the multiplication (times) table for that number.

Example

The first six multiples of 5 are: 5   10   15   20   25   30
The first six multiples of 22 are: 22   44   66   88   110   132

- Problems involving factors or multiples can be presented in real-life situations, however the calculation is just the same.

Example

A number 11 bus arrives at the depot every 20 minutes. A number 6 bus arrives at the depot every 50 minutes. If they both arrive at the depot at 9 a.m., at what time will they next arrive together?

The easiest way to tackle this question is to write out the multiples as a multiplication table. You are working in minutes, so remember that 60 minutes make an hour.

Bus number 11: 09.00   09.20   09.40   10.00   10.20   (10.40)
Bus number 6: 09.00   09.50   (10.40)
The answer is **10.40**

Finding Common Multiples and Factors

- Different numbers can have factors that are the same. These are called 'common factors'.
- The highest common factor (HCF) is the highest number that divides exactly into all the numbers listed.

Example

What is the HCF of these four numbers?   24   36   48   60
The HCF is **12**.

- Different multiplication tables can also have numbers in common. These are called 'common multiples'.

Example

What is the least common multiple (LCM) of 3 and 4?

Multiples of 3:   3, 6, 9, (12), 15, 18, 21, (24), 27, 30, 33, (36), etc.
Multiples of 4:   4, 8, (12), 16, 20, (24), 28, 32, (36), etc.

The common multiples of 3 and 4 are: 12, 24, 36, etc.
The least (i.e. the lowest) common multiple is therefore **12**.

Square and Cube Numbers

- Square numbers are found by multiplying a number by itself (also known as squaring it).
- They are called square numbers because each of the numbers could be represented by dots in a square pattern (see right).

1
1 x 1

4
2 x 2

9
3 x 3

16
4 x 4
...

- The square numbers form a sequence. Looking at the diagram to the right, the next square number can be found by squaring 5 (5 × 5 = 25) or it can be found by adding 9 to the previous square number (16 + 9 = 25).

- Cube numbers can be represented by a sequence of cubes. As shown, the cube numbers can be calculated by cubing a number, i.e. multiplying the same number by itself twice.

1 × 1 × 1 = 1   2 × 2 × 2 = 8

Problem Solving

- **Number machines** are a set of instructions that show the steps in a calculation that change the input number (the one you start with) into the output (the number at the end). Using inverse operations enables you to operate the number machine 'in reverse'.

3 × 3 × 3 = 27   4 × 4 × 4 = 64

Example
Jessica sets up a number machine as shown below.

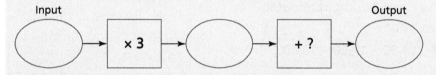

When she inputs 1, the answer is 29. What would the input number be if Jessica's machine gave an output of 50?

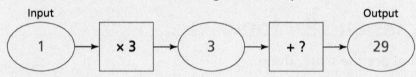

If 1 is input, the middle value is 3. 29 – 3 = 26 so the number machine adds 26.

Now use the inverse operations through the machine to find the answer.

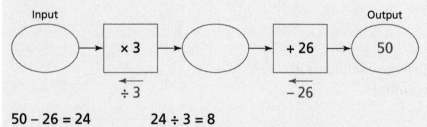

50 – 26 = 24   24 ÷ 3 = 8

The input was **8**.

- You might be presented with an incomplete grid, for example three squares wide by three squares long, where each row and each column must add up to the same value.

Example

This magic square has some empty spaces. When every space is filled in, each row and each column adds up to 27.
What number should be in the space with the question mark?

8		10	→ 27
12	?		→ 27
		7	→ 27

↓ ↓ ↓

27 27 27

Start with the rows or columns that have just one missing number:
The top row: 8 + ☐ + 10 = 27, so the missing number in the top row must be 9.
The first column: 8 + 12 + ☐ = 27, so the missing number in the bottom left square is 7.
Now the remaining empty space in the bottom row can be filled:
7 + ☐ + 7 = 27, so the missing number in the bottom row of the second column must be 13.
So the missing number in the space marked ? is: 9 + ☐ + 13 = 27, giving an answer of 5.
The fully-completed square is shown right.

8	9	10	→ 27
12	5	10	→ 27
7	13	7	→ 27

↓ ↓ ↓

27 27 27

- You may need to work out a problem to find a mystery number.

Example

Hassan is thinking of a number. He divides his number by 25 and the answer is a whole number. Which of these could be his number?

A 710   B 715   C 720   D 725   E 730

If Hassan's answer is a whole number, the number he has thought of must be a multiple of 25:

25 × 1 = 25, 25 × 2 = 50, 25 × 3 = 75, 25 × 4 = 100,
25 × 5 = 125, 25 × 6 = 150, 25 × 7 = 175, 25 × 8 = 200, etc.

We can see that each multiple ends in the digits 25, 50, 75 or 00. Only one of the options, **725**, fits into this pattern of digits so the answer is **D**.

> **Remember**
>
> Always think about what you know and use your mathematical toolbox to help you fill in the gaps to solve the problem.

Quick Test

1. Which of these lists contains only multiples of 4 or 5?
   A 12, 14, 15   B 8, 12, 13   C 8, 9, 10   D 8, 10, 11   E 12, 15, 16
2. How many factors of 36 are also square numbers?
3. One lighthouse flashes every 45 seconds. Another flashes every 50 seconds. If they flash together at exactly 9 p.m., how many seconds will pass before they flash together again?
4. A magic square is shown in which each row and each column sums to the same total. It contains the even numbers from 4 to 20. Complete the square.

10		
8		16
		14

5. I am thinking of a number. I multiply it by 6 and add 3 to the answer. I then subtract 8 and the final answer is 55. What was my original number?

Fractions, Decimals and Percentages

You should be able to:

- calculate with fractions, decimals and percentages
- find equivalent fractions, decimals and percentages
- calculate probabilities using fractions, decimals and percentages.

Comparing and Ordering Fractions

- To generate equivalent fractions, write out the fraction then multiply the numerator and the denominator by the same value.

Example

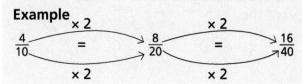

- To find a fraction in its lowest terms, divide the numerator and the denominator by the highest common factor (HCF).

Example

Express $\frac{16}{40}$ in its lowest terms.

The HCF of the numerator and the denominator is 8.

$16 \div 8 = 2$ $40 \div 8 = 5$

$\frac{2}{5}$ is the fraction in its lowest terms.

- To write a set of fractions in order quickly, adjust the fractions so that the denominators are all the same value:
  - The common denominator will be a common multiple.
  - For simplicity, work with the lowest common multiple.

Example

Order these fractions, starting with the smallest:

$\frac{1}{2}$ $\frac{5}{6}$ $\frac{3}{4}$ $\frac{7}{12}$ $\frac{2}{3}$

Find the lowest common multiple. This is 12. Change all the fractions to twelfths (whichever number you multiply the denominator by to get 12, you do the same for the numerator):

$\frac{6}{12}$ $\frac{10}{12}$ $\frac{9}{12}$ $\frac{7}{12}$ $\frac{8}{12}$

Now order the fractions by the numerators, starting with the smallest:

$\frac{6}{12}$ $\frac{7}{12}$ $\frac{8}{12}$ $\frac{9}{12}$ $\frac{10}{12}$

In the original format: $\frac{1}{2}$ $\frac{7}{12}$ $\frac{2}{3}$ $\frac{3}{4}$ $\frac{5}{6}$

- To simplify or write an improper fraction as a mixed number, it is useful to know your times tables to identify multiples quickly. You first need to find the whole number.

Example

What is $\frac{74}{8}$ as a mixed number in its lowest terms?

To write this number in its lowest terms, see how many times 8 fits into 74: $8 \times 9 = 72$

This makes 9 the whole number and the fraction left is $\frac{2}{8}$, which can then be simplified to $\frac{1}{4}$.

So $\frac{74}{8} = 9\frac{1}{4}$

Adding and Subtracting Fractions

- The process for adding and subtracting fractions begins in the same way as for ordering fractions – change the denominators to a common number. Once the denominators are the same, you can then add or subtract the numerators.

Example

$$\frac{2}{3} - \frac{1}{6} \quad = \quad \frac{4}{6} - \frac{1}{6} \quad = \quad \frac{3}{6}$$

Simplify the fraction to its lowest terms to find the answer.

$$\frac{3}{6} = \frac{1}{2}$$

Remember

Don't add or subtract the denominators.

Multiplying and Dividing Fractions

- The first step in multiplying and dividing fractions is to make sure they are not written as mixed numbers.
- To multiply, write as a single fraction where the numerators are multiplied by each other and the denominators are multiplied by each other. Before doing the multiplications, you can look for common factors and simplify if possible.

Example

$$\frac{2}{3} \times \frac{5}{6} \quad = \quad \frac{2 \times 5}{3 \times 6} \quad = \quad \frac{1 \times 5}{3 \times 3} \quad = \quad \frac{5}{9}$$

Remember

Always check if the final answer can be simplified any further.

- To divide, use the fact that multiplication and division are inverse operations. For example, multiplying by $\frac{1}{4}$ is the same as dividing by 4, so dividing by $\frac{1}{4}$ is the same as multiplying by 4.
- Dividing by a fraction is the same as multiplying by its inverse. For example, dividing by $\frac{5}{7}$ is the same as multiplying by $\frac{7}{5}$.
- Convert any mixed numbers to improper fractions before you carry out the operation.

Example

$$1\frac{3}{5} \div 1\frac{1}{15} \quad = \quad \frac{8}{5} \div \frac{16}{15} \quad = \quad \frac{8}{5} \times \frac{15}{16}$$

$$= \quad \frac{8 \times 15}{5 \times 16} \quad = \quad \frac{1 \times 3}{1 \times 2}$$

$$= \quad \frac{3}{2} \quad = \quad 1\frac{1}{2}$$

Calculating Fractions of an Amount

- Use division to find a simple fraction of a given amount.
  So, to find $\frac{1}{3}$ of £27, divide £27 by the denominator 3.
- To find a fraction with a numerator greater than 1, you also
  need to multiply. To find $\frac{2}{3}$ of £27, divide £27 by 3 and multiply
  by the numerator 2.
- To find out the total amount from a fraction, both division and
  multiplication are needed again.

Example

If 30 grams is $\frac{3}{5}$ the weight of a box of pencils, what is the total weight of the box?

You need to find out what one part ($\frac{1}{5}$) of the amount equals first.
So divide 30 grams by the numerator to find the value of $\frac{1}{5}$, then multiply by
the denominator to find the total weight.

$30\,g \div 3 = 10\,g$ $10\,g \times 5 = \textbf{50\,g}$

- When you calculate fractions of real-life things, a diagram
  can help.

Example

If five pizzas are shared between six children, what fraction of a pizza does each child get?

Begin by working out how much of a single pizza each child would receive. To do this you need to
divide one pizza into six, i.e. one piece for each child.

You now know that a child will have $\frac{1}{6}$ of a single pizza, so this makes it easier to
calculate the fraction they would receive from five pizzas.

$\frac{1}{6} \times 5 = \frac{5}{6}$, so each child will receive $\frac{5}{6}$ of a pizza.

- Some probability questions are fraction questions in disguise.

Example

What is the probability of throwing an even number on a regular, six-sided dice?

There are six possible numbers. The denominator is 6.

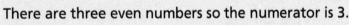
1   2   3   4   5   6

There are three even numbers so the numerator is 3.

Therefore the probability is $\frac{3}{6}$ or $\frac{1}{2}$.

> **Quick Test**

1. Put these fractions in order of size from smallest to largest: $\frac{11}{20}$ $\frac{4}{5}$ $\frac{1}{2}$ $\frac{3}{4}$ $\frac{7}{10}$

2. Which pair of these fractions add up to one whole? $\frac{5}{8}$ $\frac{2}{8}$ $\frac{1}{2}$ $\frac{3}{4}$ $\frac{7}{8}$

3. Write $4\frac{3}{8}$ as an improper fraction.

4. What fraction of the numbers in this list are **prime**? 1, 3, 5, 7, 9, 11, 13, 15, 17

5. Sunita spent £56 on some new trainers. After this she had $\frac{3}{10}$ of her money left.
   How much money does she have left?

6. Eric eats $\frac{2}{3}$ of a bag of sweets. Joanna eats $\frac{2}{3}$ of what is left, then Zoltan eats $\frac{2}{3}$ of what Joanna
   left. There are now 2 sweets in the bag. How many were there to start with?

Equivalent Fractions, Decimals and Percentages

- **Fractions** can also be written as a decimal or a percentage.
- **Decimals** can be written as fractions with a denominator that is a power of 10 (10, 100, 1,000, etc.).
- To find a numerical fraction from a decimal, write it as a fraction, with the number of zeros to match the number of figures after the decimal point.

Example

$0.3 = \frac{3}{10}$ $0.03 = \frac{3}{100}$ $0.34 = \frac{34}{100}$

Check to see if the fractions can be simplified:

$0.3 = \frac{3}{10}$ $0.03 = \frac{3}{100}$ $0.34 = \frac{34}{100} = \frac{17}{50}$

- **Percentages** are fractions with a denominator of 100, such as:
  $1\% = \frac{1}{100}$ and $15\% = \frac{15}{100}$
- Percentages are not always whole numbers:
  $12.5\% = \frac{12.5}{100} = \frac{25}{200} = \frac{1}{8}$
- Percentages can be converted into decimals by dividing by 100 (move the digits two places to the right); so $12.5\% = 0.125$
- Learning the equivalents in the table by heart will help you work at speed.

Fraction	Decimal	Percentage
1	1.0	100%
$\frac{1}{2}$	0.5	50%
$\frac{1}{4}$	0.25	25%
$\frac{3}{4}$	0.75	75%
$\frac{1}{10}$	0.1	10%
$\frac{1}{5}$	0.2	20%
$\frac{1}{100}$	0.01	1%

- When you are asked to compare fractions with decimals or percentages, convert all the values to the same format to make them easier to compare.
- In the following example, converting all the values to decimals makes it easier to find the correct answer.

Example

Which of the following statements is correct?

A $2.25 = 2\frac{25}{10}$ **B** $2.25 = 2\frac{25}{50}$ **C** $2.25 = 2\frac{1}{4}$ **D** $2.25 = 2\frac{225}{100}$ **E** $2.25 = 22.5\%$

Change all the values to decimals:

A $2\frac{25}{10} = 2 + 2.5 = 4.5$ **B** $2\frac{25}{50} = 2 + \frac{50}{100} = 2.5$ **C** $2\frac{1}{4} = 2 + \frac{25}{100} = 2.25$

D $2\frac{225}{100} = 2 + 2 + \frac{25}{100} = 4.25$ **E** $22.5\% = 0.225$

Option **C** is the correct answer.

Comparing and Ordering Decimals

- Ordering decimals is an extension of ordering whole numbers (see page 7).
- To order a group of decimal numbers such as 1, 0.1, 0.01, 11.001, 1.023:
    - write the numbers in a vertical list, lining up the decimal points
    - fill in any gaps with zeros, as place holders, to avoid errors.
- Now the numbers can be easily ordered: 11.001, 1.023, 1, 0.1, 0.01

tens	ones (units)	decimal point	tenths	hundredths	thousandths
0	1	.	0	0	0
0	0	.	1	0	0
0	0	.	0	1	0
1	1	.	0	0	1
0	1	.	0	2	3

Calculations with Decimals

- When **adding** and **subtracting** decimals, line up the decimal points and insert any missing zeros as place holders, as shown right.
- Complete in the same way as a whole number addition or subtraction sum, remembering to keep the decimal point in the answer below the decimal point in the calculation.
- To **multiply** decimals, you can use your knowledge of division by 10s, or you can use estimation.

```
    2 . 0 2 1
 +  3 . 2 0 0
 ─────────────
    5 . 2 2 1
```

Example

$4.1 \times 0.9 = ?$

$4.1 \times 0.9 = (41 \div 10) \times (9 \div 10) = 41 \times 9 \div 10 \div 10 = 369 \div 100 =$ **3.69**

Or

$41 \times 9 = 369$

$4.1 \times 0.9 \approx 4 \times 1 = 4$

So answer = **3.69**

- To **divide** decimals, you should make the number you are dividing by into a whole number.

Example

$2.79 \div 0.9 = ?$

Multiply both numbers by 10 (this is like equivalent fractions; what you do to one number you must do to the other): $27.9 \div 9$

You can now calculate the answer: **3.1**

Rounding Decimals

- Rounding decimals can help you to estimate answers to check your calculations.
- Rounding to one decimal place means rounding to the nearest 0.1 or $\frac{1}{10}$, so 12.74 rounded to one decimal place is 12.7
- Rounding to two decimal places means rounding to the nearest $\frac{1}{100}$, so 1.275 rounded to two decimal places is 1.28

Simple Probability

- Probability is how likely that something (an 'outcome') will happen.
- The probability that an outcome **will** happen and the probability it **will not** happen always add up to 1.
- You can describe the outcome with words such as impossible, unlikely, even chance, certain.
- You can also describe the outcome using numbers:
  - **Impossible** is represented by 0
  - **Even chance** is represented by 0.5
  - **Certain** is represented by 1.
- When you flip a coin, there are two possible outcomes. The possibility of flipping a head will be one chance in two. You can represent this as the fraction $\frac{1}{2}$, the decimal 0.5, or the percentage 50%.
- You can use probabilities to estimate how many times an outcome will happen.

Calculating Probability with Fractions

- To calculate a probability when all the outcomes are equally likely is straightforward. Simply add up the number of different outcomes and the total will be the fraction's denominator and the numerator will be 1.
- When the outcomes are not equally likely, calculate them as a numerical fraction, as follows.

Example

In a paper bag there are 4 strawberry, 3 orange, 2 lemon and 1 blackberry sweets. What is the probability of picking out a strawberry sweet?

First you need to work out the total number of sweets. Add together the numbers of each flavour sweet: 4 + 3 + 2 + 1 = 10
This provides the denominator for a fraction. Then each number of sweets provides the numerators.
The probability of picking a strawberry sweet is: $\frac{4}{10} = \frac{2}{5}$

Calculating Probability with Decimals and Percentages

- Probability can also be represented by decimals and percentages.

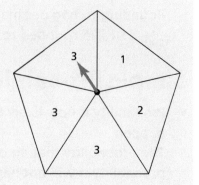

Example

What is the probability of this spinner landing on a 3?

There are five equal sections; the probability of landing on each of these equals 0.2.

Count the number of sections that have the number 3. There are three sections, so: 0.2 × 3 = 0.6

The probability of the spinner landing on 3 is **0.6** (or, as a percentage, **60%**).

Problem Solving

- A number machine can be a good way to help visualise a multi-step fractions problem.

Example

A number machine is set up as follows:

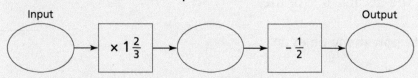

A number 2 is placed in the input. What will the output be?

$$1\frac{2}{3} = \frac{1 \times 3 + 2}{3} = \frac{5}{3}$$

$$\frac{2}{1} \times \frac{5}{3} = \frac{2 \times 5}{1 \times 3} = \frac{10}{3} \quad \boxed{\text{work out} \times 1\frac{2}{3}}$$

$$\frac{10}{3} - \frac{1}{2} = \frac{20}{6} - \frac{3}{6} \quad \boxed{\text{work out} - \frac{1}{2}}$$

$$\frac{20 - 3}{6} = \frac{17}{6} = \mathbf{2\frac{5}{6}}$$

- The context can vary, so try to look beyond the words to see the mathematics and pick out the calculation to be done.

Example

Boris has a bag containing 56 marbles. The marbles are either red, green, or blue. $\frac{3}{7}$ of the marbles are red. 25% of the remaining marbles are green. What is the probability of getting a blue marble if picked randomly from the bag?

$\frac{3}{7}$ of 56 = 56 ÷ 7 × 3 = 24   There are 24 red marbles.

56 − 24 = 32   There are 32 marbles that are either green or blue.

25% of 32 = 32 ÷ 4 = 8   There are 8 green marbles.

32 − 8 = 24   There are 24 blue marbles.
       (Check: 24 + 8 + 24 = 56)

There are 24 blue marbles out of a total 56 marbles, so the blue marbles are $\frac{24}{56} = \frac{3}{7}$ of the whole bag (this is the same as the proportion of red marbles).

The probability of randomly picking a blue marble is $\frac{3}{7}$.

Quick Test

1. Find the smallest of these quantities.

   A 1.8%   B 0.18   C $\frac{1}{18}$ D 0.081   E 0.108

2. Which of these is closest to 1?

   A 0.99   B 95%   C 1.05   D 103%   E $\frac{49}{50}$

3. Which of these does not have the same value as the others?

   A $\frac{1}{5}$ B 0.2   C 2%   D $\frac{2}{10}$ E $\frac{5}{25}$

4. What percentage of this grid is shaded?

5. This spinner is equally likely to land on any of the numbers 1, 4, 9, 16 or 25. What is the probability that it will land on an odd number?

Ratio and Proportion

You should be able to:

- work out equivalent ratios
- divide numbers and quantities into a given ratio
- use proportional reasoning to solve problems
- solve percentage problems.

Ratios and Equivalent Ratios

- Ratios are a way of comparing numbers and quantities.
- A ratio shows proportion in a different way to a fraction.
- When you mix paint one part white to four parts blue, you write it as a ratio 1:4 so there is a total of five 'parts'. One part is white and four parts are blue. So the fraction of white paint is $\frac{1}{5}$ and the fraction of blue paint is $\frac{4}{5}$.
- As with fractions, where the denominator and numerator are multiplied or divided by the same number, the same rule applies to ratios:
  - These equivalent fractions are all produced by multiplying by 2: $\frac{1}{2} = \frac{2}{4} = \frac{4}{8}$
  - These equivalent ratios are all produced by multiplying by 2: $2:3 = 4:6 = 8:12$

Remember

In ratios, always check which way round the numbers go. If two teaspoons of chilli are used to 100 g of mince, don't add 100 g of chilli to two teaspoons of mince!

Scales on Maps

- Maps, models and plans use scaling to enable something big to be represented on something much smaller.
- Maps, models and plans use space and distance on a smaller scale than in real life, but the relative position of objects stays the same. So a distance that is twice as long as another distance in real life will still be twice as long on the map.
- Scales are given as a ratio. A 1:500 ratio means that 1 centimetre on the map represents 500 cm (or 5 metres) in real life.

Remember

If given a measurement on a map, multiply to find the real distance.

If given a distance in real life, divide to find the distance on the map.

Example

Gwen draws a map to show her route to school. She uses a scale of 1:40,000.

a) Her school is 2 km away from her house. How far will it be on the map?

2 km = 2,000 m = 200,000 cm   200,000 cm ÷ 40,000 = 5 cm

On the map the school will be **5 cm** away.

b) Gwen has put a spot on the map where the swimming pool is. On the map the distance from her house to the swimming pool is 8.5 cm. How far away is it in real life?

8.5 cm × 40,000 = 340,000 cm

(this isn't very useful as it is hard to understand how far 340,000 cm is)

340,000 cm = 3,400 m = 3.4 km

In real life the swimming pool is **3.4 km** away.

Proportion

- You can divide numbers and quantities into a given ratio.
  First you need to work out how many parts there are in total.

Example

A field contains 28 llamas. These are then split between two fields in a ratio of
2:5. How many llamas are in each field?

To solve this problem:
- there are seven (2 + 5) equal 'groups' of llamas
- to find out how many in a group, divide the total number by the number
  of groups: $28 \div 7 = 4$
- to finish the problem, multiply this figure by the number of groups on
  each side of the ratio.
  $4 \times 2 = 8$ $4 \times 5 = 20$

The number of llamas in each field is **8** and **20**.

- Knowing the proportions of one quantity to another means
  that if one quantity changes, you can work out the other.

Example

In a recipe you need two eggs to every 300 g of sugar. How many eggs will you
need if the recipe asks for 1,200 g of sugar?

To solve this problem:
- first look for the proportions you are dealing with
  2:300 is the ratio of eggs to sugar (in grams)   ?:1,200
- you now need to work out how many times bigger 1,200 is than 300: $1,200 \div 300 = 4$
- so to calculate the new quantity, multiply the original number of eggs by 4:   2:300 × 4

The answer is **8** eggs.

Percentage Calculations

- Some percentage calculations are quite simple if you look for
  alternative methods to solve them. Using equivalents by converting
  a percentage to a fraction can speed up your calculations.

Example

Find 10% of £350.

10% is the same as $\frac{1}{10}$

So 10% of £350 equals **£35**.

- Working backwards can help solve some questions. In this case,
  you don't need to convert the percentage to a fraction; just
  look for simple fractions.

Example

Find 75% of £350.

Find half (50%) of £350, then find half of this half (25%),
then add the two together:

£350 ÷ 2 = £175   £175 ÷ 2 = £87.50

£175 + £87.50 = **£262.50**

- Use multiplication and division to solve percentage problems when you know the total amount.
- If you can find 1% of an amount, you can multiply this value to find any percentage. To find 1% you need to divide the number by 100 – move the digits two places to the right. So 1% of £451 is £4.51
- To find 10% of any number, move the digits one place to the right. So 10% of £451 is £45.10
- Once you know 1% and 10%, many calculations are simple. So 5% of £451 is £45.10 ÷ 2 = £22.55

Example

Find 14% of £451.

Either multiply 14 by 1%: £4.51 × 14 = **£63.14**

Or add 10% and 5% and subtract 1%:

£45.10 + £22.55 – £4.51 = **£63.14**

- You can also use multiplication and division to solve percentage problems when you need to find the total amount.

Example

48 children stay for homework club after school. If this is 24% of the school, how many children are in the whole school?

To solve this, you still need to find 1%. If 48 children are 24% of the school, to find 1% divide 48 by 24:

48 ÷ 24 = 2

Then multiply this by 100:   2 × 100 = 200

So there are **200** children in the school.

Quick Test

1. Which of these ratios is not equivalent to 16 : 12?
   A 20 : 15   B 8 : 6   C 24 : 16   D 36 : 27   E 32 : 24
2. In a choir, the ratio of boys to girls is 5 : 3. There are 18 girls in the choir.
   How many children are in the choir altogether?
3. Will has just finished building a model plane with a scale of 1 : 72. The model is 20 cm long.
   How long is the real plane in metres?
4. St Mark's School sold 500 tickets for a raffle. 4% of the tickets won a prize.
   How many tickets did not win a prize?
5. Which answer is different from the others?
   A 50% of £50   B 25% of £100   C $\frac{5}{8}$ of £40   D 30% of £75   E 10% of £250
6. A jar of jam used to cost £1.20 but the price has increased by 20%.
   What does it cost now?

Algebra

You should be able to:

- understand and use algebraic notation
- solve equations
- understand sequences and work out missing patterns or terms
- work out how many different combinations are possible in a given situation.

Understanding Algebraic Notation

- You need to know how additions, subtractions, multiplications and divisions are written in algebra.
- To add and subtract, write the letters as you would do for numbers in a calculation.

Example
Adding a to b: $a + b =$
Subtracting a from b: $b - a =$

- Multiplication sums do not use signs; the numbers and letters are written next to each other.

Example
$4x$ is four times the value of x, so if $x = 6$ then:
$4x = 4 \times 6 = \mathbf{24}$

- Division sums are usually shown like numerical fractions.

Example
$\frac{k}{10}$ means the number represented by k should be divided by 10.
So if $k = 40$, then:
$\frac{k}{10} = \frac{40}{10} = 40 \div 10 = \mathbf{4}$

Using Substitution and Solving Equations

- Substituting letters for unknown numbers helps to solve equations.

Example
$8 + ? + ? = 26$
There are a variety of answers that could be correct.
$8 + 1 + 17 = 26$ $8 + 2 + 16 = 26$
$8 + 3 + 15 = 26$ $8 + 4 + 14 = 26$
$8 + 5 + 13 = 26$ $8 + 6 + 12 = 26$, etc.
Using letters to replace the ?: $8 + a + a = 26$
You can then work out the value of a. You will also understand that a needs to have the same value each time it occurs within this equation. So $a = \mathbf{9}$.

- You can solve equations in two different ways – by simplifying the sums until you find the answer, or by using number machines.

Simplifying the Sum

- To solve equations by simplifying the sum, you need to move the numbers you know to one side of the equation, leaving the calculations involving letters you don't know on the other side.
- You can move a number from one side of the equation to the other by using inverse operations.

> **Example**
>
> $k = 3s + 4$
>
> If you know $k = 19$, you can work out the value of s:
>
> $19 = 3s + 4$
>
> $19 - 4 = 3s$
>
> $15 = 3s$
>
> $15 \div 3 = s$, so $s = 5$

Remember

The unknown value can occur more than once in the equation, e.g.

$2x + 3 = x + 7$

$(x = 4)$

And the answer can be a fraction:

$16x = 4$

$x = \frac{1}{4}$

Using Number Machines

- Use inverse operations when you work backwards.

> **Example**
>
> Look at this number machine for the equation $\frac{4b + 4}{2} = 12$
>
> What is the value of b?
>
>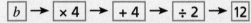
>
> First change the direction and the operations:
>
> $\boxed{b} \leftarrow \boxed{\div 4} \leftarrow \boxed{- 4} \leftarrow \boxed{\times 2} \leftarrow \boxed{12}$
>
> Then complete the operations: $b = 5$

Remember

Make sure you change the operation when you change direction.

Recognising Sequences

- You need to be able to spot number sequences quickly.
- Odd and even numbers:
  - Both odd and even number sequences have a difference of 2 each time.
  - Even numbers are all multiples of 2.

  1   2   3   4   5   6   7   8   9   10   ...

- Sequences from multiplication tables:
  - Equal differences indicate a repeated addition sequence.

    6   12   18   24

        +6   +6   +6

  - Increasing differences can indicate a sequence linked by multiplication. This pattern shows multiplication by 2.

    2   4   8   16

        +2   +4   +8

  - Decreasing numbers can indicate repeated subtraction or division.

- Make sure you can recognise sequences of square and cube numbers:

  | Square numbers: | 1 | 4 | 9 | 16 | 25 | 36 | ... |
  | Cube numbers: | 1 | 8 | 27 | 64 | 125 | 216 | ... |

- Triangular numbers start at 1 and then add 2, 3, 4 progressively. The differences are consecutive numbers.

  | 1 | 3 | 6 | 10 | 15 | 21 | ... |

- Prime numbers are only divisible by 1 and themselves; there is no pattern to them.

  | 2 | 3 | 5 | 7 | 11 | 13 | ... |

- If the sequence is not easy to recognise, look at the differences between the numbers. This can help to identify patterns.

  | 7 | | 8 | | 11 | | 16 | | 23 |
  | | +1 | | +3 | | +5 | | +7 | |

- Look out for sequences that go backwards as well as forwards.

Completing and Extending Sequences

- First check the pattern in the sequence by looking at the differences between your given numbers.

Example

Work out the missing number in this sequence:

| 8 | 16 | ___ | 32 | 40 | 48 |

The example here is a positive number sequence. The difference between the given numbers is always 8.

Work out the difference between the terms given, then add/subtract this to a number next to the gap.

Check that your answer fits the sequence correctly.

Here 16 + 8 or 32 − 8 will give the correct answer of **24**.

Remember

If the sequence is negative, the process shown in the example to the left is reversed.

Shape-based Patterns

- Identify what stays the same in the pattern and what changes.

Example

What is the next shape in the series?

o   o   o   o
o   oo   ooo oooo

First find the things that stay the same. Here these are the shape and the top row.

Then find out the element that changes: one circle is added to the bottom row each time.

So the next shape is: o
        ooooo

1. Two years ago, Joyti's brother was y years old. How old will he be in five years' time?
   A $y + 7$ B $y - 7$ C $y + 5$ D $y + 3$ E $y - 2$
2. What is the value of x, if $6x + 4 = 2x + 10$?
3. Find the next number in this sequence:
   5, 9, 17, 33, 65, 129, ...
4. How many matchsticks are needed to make the next pattern in the sequence?

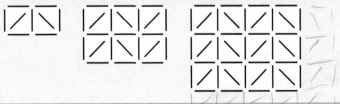

Two Unknowns

- When dealing with a situation where there are two unknown values, try to set up equations with the information that is given.
- You may be able to rule out some multiple-choice options straight away and then test the others.

Example

James is making button pictures. Each rainbow picture he makes uses 10 red buttons. Each fish picture he makes has 6 red buttons. He makes p rainbow pictures and enjoys making the fish pictures even more so makes q fish pictures. He started with 50 red buttons but only has 6 left when he is finished. Which is the correct solution?

A $p = 2, q = 1$ B $p = 3, q = 5$ C $p = 2, q = 4$

D $p = 3, q = 3$ E $p = 1, q = 6$

Start by writing down the information from the question mathematically.

$q > p$ q is bigger than p

$10p + 6q = 50 - 6 = 44$

Using this information, test the answer options:
It is not **A** or **D**, because q is not bigger than p in those answers.

Try **B**: $10 \times 3 + 6 \times 5 = 60$ This is not the right answer; we want it to be 44.

Try **C**: $10 \times 2 + 6 \times 4 = 44$ This is the right answer.

Try **E**: $10 \times 1 + 6 \times 6 = 46$ This is close but not right – this way he would only have 4 buttons left.

Option **C** is correct.

Combinations and Permutations

- Combinations and permutations are all about how many different ways a set of items can be put together.
- Often the best way to attempt these questions is to write down one item (use a code, like the first letter, to make it easier to do) and then all the things that could go with it. The question will explain how the matching up can happen.

Example
A café offers the sandwich fillings shown on the right.
How many different options are there for a sandwich with two fillings?

Sandwich fillings
Ham
Cheese
Tuna mayonnaise
Salad
Hummus
Add a second filling for 50p!

> Ham (H), Cheese (C), Tuna (T), Salad (S), Hummus (M)

There are the following possible combinations:

HC	CT	TS	SM
HT	CS	TM	(SC = CS, SH = HS, ST = TS, so all covered)
HS	CM	(Tuna with either Ham or Cheese is already covered)	
HM	(CH = HC so is not included again)		

There are **10** possible combinations.

Notice that if there are five items on the list, the first item could match with all four of the other items. The second item matches with the three remaining items but has already been matched with the first item, etc. So for five items to be arranged into different pairs the calculation becomes 4 + 3 + 2 + 1 = 10. Sometimes it might be possible to have two of the same, so in this situation you might get HH, CC, TT, SS, MM.

- Sometimes there will be two lists so each item from one list can go with one item from the second list.

Example
A café offers a (single filling) sandwich with a piece of fruit as part of a meal deal. How many different combinations of sandwich and fruit are possible?

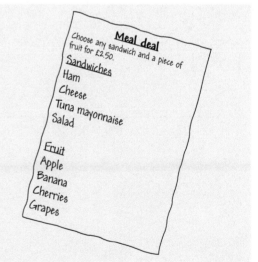

Meal deal
Choose any sandwich and a piece of fruit for £2.50.
Sandwiches
Ham
Cheese
Tuna mayonnaise
Salad

Fruit
Apple
Banana
Cherries
Grapes

List the possible combinations:

HA	CA	TA	SA
HB	CB	TB	SB
HC	CC	TC	SC
HG	CG	TG	SG

Counting up there are **16** possible combinations.

- The answer above is set out as a grid with each item from the first list having a column and each item from the second list having a row. This means the number of possible combinations is 4 × 4 = 16. If there were 5 sandwich filling options and 6 types of fruit, the number of combinations would be 30. Can you see why?

- In both of the previous examples, the order of the items doesn't matter – they are **combinations**.
- **Permutations** are when the order does matter, for example the numbers on the code for a safe. If you knew it had the digits 390 but didn't know the order, that still leaves a lot of different numbers. Sometimes digits or items can be repeated but sometimes they cannot – think about the practical situation to decide.

> **Remember**
>
> Make sure you have a system when listing outcomes. Start with the first and list all the possible things that could go with it, then move on to the second. Grids can be a helpful way of keeping track of what you have done and help you to spot patterns.

Example

Four people (Anand, Beatrice, Charlie, Damien) are running a race. How many different permutations could there be for the medal positions (i.e. the first three places)?

List the first three in order of finishing. Have a system: here the columns have the same pair first, and they are always done from earlier in the alphabet first.

ABC	ACB	ADB	BAC	BCA	BDA
ABD	ACD	ADC	BAD	BCD	BDC

Having got this far it is possible to spot a pattern, which can save you writing out all the different permutations. For each different person in first place there are six possible permutations for the remaining runners.

So, there are $4 \times 6 = 24$ permutations for the medal positions.

Quick Test

1. Maya is planting sunflower seeds. She plants m seeds in each small pot and n seeds in each big pot. When she has planted 4 of each size pot, she has 4 seeds left over from a packet of 20.
   Which is correct?
   A $m = 2, n = 1$ B $m = 3, n = 2$ C $m = 2, n = 3$ D $m = 1, n = 4$ E $m = 1, n = 3$

2. When playing a game, these two spinners are spun at the same time and the two values obtained are added together.
   How many different combinations of totals are there?

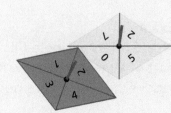

Measurement

You should be able to:
- understand and use measures such as money, time, temperature, speed, length, capacity and mass (weight)
- convert between different units of measurement
- calculate the area, volume and perimeter of different shapes.

Money

- Money is measured in pounds (£) and pence (p).
- There are 100 pence in £1, so 3p written in pounds would be represented in the hundredths column, i.e. £0.03.
- We have these coins and notes in the UK: 1p, 2p, 5p, 10p, 20p, 50p, £1, £2, £5, £10, £20, £50.
- You can make any amount of money from the coins and notes.

Example
Gareth has these coins:

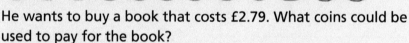

He wants to buy a book that costs £2.79. What coins could be used to pay for the book?

Using the two £1 coins leaves £0.79 or 79p to pay.

Using the 50p piece leaves 29p.

Using a 20p piece leaves 9p.

Using the 5p piece leaves 4p, which can be made using the 2p and 2 × 1p.

£2.79 = £1 + £1 + 50p + 20p + 5p + 2p + 1p + 1p

- You need to be able to calculate using money.

Example
Misa gets two 20 pence pieces for pocket money every week. She puts them in her money box. After how many weeks will she have more than £5?

It is easier to work in pence here:

£5 = 500p and Misa gets 40p each week.

500 ÷ 40 = 50 ÷ 4 = 25 ÷ 2 = 12.5

Now round up 12.5 to the next whole week.

So it will take **13** weeks for Misa to have more than £5 in her money box.

Time

- If you are working with the 12-hour clock, you need to understand a.m. and p.m. For example, 9.34 a.m. is in the morning and 9.34 p.m. is in the evening.
- If you are working with the 24-hour clock, you always use four numbers. So 09:34 indicates the time is in the morning, while 21:34 is in the evening (9.34 p.m.).
- When converting 12-hour clock times to 24-hour clock times, take care when dealing with times from 12 midnight (00:00 on the 24-hour clock) to 12.59 a.m. (00:59).
- When asked to work out the difference between two times (a time interval), it is useful to quickly draw a timeline.
- If the time interval crosses 12 noon or 12 midnight, you can use extra steps to make the calculation easier.

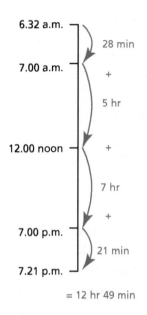

6.32 a.m.
28 min
7.00 a.m.
+
5 hr
12.00 noon
+
7 hr
+
7.00 p.m.
21 min
7.21 p.m.

= 12 hr 49 min

Calculating with Time and Using Timetables

- To calculate using time, you need to know the units used to measure time:

1 millennium	1,000 years
1 century	100 years
1 decade	10 years
1 year	12 months or 365 days (but 366 days in a leap year)
1 day	24 hours
1 hour	60 minutes
1 minute	60 seconds

- To remember how many days there are in each month, you can use your knuckles.
- The raised knuckles have 31 days, and the indents between the knuckles have 30 days, except for February, which has 28 days (but has 29 days in a leap year).

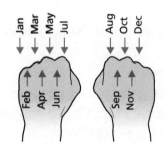

Jan Mar May Jul   Aug Oct Dec

Feb Apr Jun   Sep Nov

Example
Tennis lessons are 45 minutes long. If Janine's grandparents offer to pay for 15 hours of lessons, how many lessons can Janine take?

There are two ways to solve this problem.
If you double 45 minutes, this makes 90 minutes
(1 hour 30 minutes) which is the time needed for 2 lessons.
4 lessons = 3 hours
Multiplying by 5 gives:
20 lessons = 15 hours
Therefore, number of lessons in 15 hours = **20**

Alternatively, you can start by calculating the total number of minutes in 15 hours:
15 hours = 15 × 60 minutes = 900 minutes
Dividing by 45 minutes per lesson gives **20** lessons.

- Timetables (bus, rail) usually use the 24-hour clock. They are displayed in columns and rows.
- Each column represents a separate journey. If there is a blank space or dash in a timetable, it means that there isn't a service at that stop.

Revision

Remember

When adding and subtracting units of time, there are 60 minutes in an hour.

Example
What is the earliest train you can catch from Jamestone to Seeford on Monday?

Station		Saturdays only		
Jamestone	05:34	07:34	08:34	13:34
Seeford		07:42	08:42	13:42
Lingtop	06:34	08:34		14:34
Strayram	06:54	08:54	09:54	14:54

The earliest train is at **08:34** (as the 07:34 only runs on a Saturday).

Temperature

- Temperature measures how warm, or cold, something is.
- The unit measure of temperature is degrees Celsius (°C).
- A thermometer is used to measure the temperature of something.
- Values below 0°C are represented by negative numbers.

Example
Emma checks the temperature in her greenhouse in August and the thermometer displays the reading shown.
On the coldest winter day, the temperature is 43°C colder. What is the temperature on the coldest day?

36 − 43 = −7, so on the coldest winter day the temperature was **−7°C**.

Units of Measure

- You need to know what unit is suitable for measuring different things and have a sense of the size of each unit.

Item	Type of Measure	Measuring Equipment	Units of Measurement
How heavy a grown up is	Weight (mass)	Bathroom scales	Kilograms (kg) (Imperial units: stones and ounces)
Size of a book	Length	Ruler	Centimetres (cm) (Imperial units: inches)
Milk	Capacity (volume)	Measuring jug	Litres (l) or millilitres (ml) (Imperial units: pints)
Size of a room	Length	Tape measure	Metres (m) (Imperial units: feet and inches)
How much flour when baking	Weight (mass)	Kitchen scales	Grams (g) (Imperial units: pounds and ounces)
Dose of medicine	Capacity (volume)	Medical syringe or measuring spoon	Millilitres (ml)
Distance of a bike ride	Length	Pedometer; measuring wheel; using an app; distance from a scaled map	Kilometres (km) (Imperial units: miles)

Converting Between Metric Units

- Metric units function on a system in base 10, which means there are set units and prefixes (the bit at the beginning of a unit) that tell us how big or small the unit is.
- The prefixes are:
  - milli- (meaning a 'thousandth'), e.g. millimetres (mm), milligrams (mg), millilitres (ml)
  - centi- (meaning a 'hundredth'), e.g. centimetres (cm), centilitres (cl)
  - kilo- (meaning 1,000 times bigger), e.g. kilometres (km), kilograms (kg).
- When multiplying or adding measures, it is sometimes more sensible to convert units.

Remember

The three standard units (known as SI units) are:

- metres (m) for length
- grams (g) for weight (or mass)
- litres (l) for capacity (or volume).

Example

Seren is building a tower with bricks that are 15 cm tall. Before toppling, the tower is 22 blocks high. What was the maximum height of Seren's tower?

A 330 m   **B** 0.33 m   **C** 3,300 m   **D** 3.3 m   **E** 33 m

$15 \times 22 = 30 \times 11 = 330$ cm

To match it to the answer, convert into metres.

$330 \div 100 = 3.3$ m (option **D**)

Check the answer makes sense. Try converting back or using an estimation to make sure, as it is very easy to make a mistake and multiply instead of divide or vice-versa.

Remember

There are:

- 1,000 millilitres (or 1,000 cm³) in a litre
- 100 cm in a metre
- 1,000 g in a kilogram
- 1,000 kg in a tonne.

- Take extra care when working with different units of area or volume:
  - $1\,m^2 = 1\,m \times 1\,m = 100\,cm \times 100\,cm = 10,000\,cm^2$
  - $1\,cm^3 = 1\,cm \times 1\,cm \times 1\,cm = 10\,mm \times 10\,mm \times 10\,mm = 1,000\,mm^3$

Imperial-to-Metric Conversions

- The most common conversions are:
  - miles to kilometres
  - pints or gallons to litres
  - pounds to kilograms.

Remember

These imperial-to-metric conversions are approximate.

Length

Imperial	1 inch	1 foot	39 inches	1 mile	5 miles
Metric	2.5 cm	30 cm	1 m	1.6 km	8 km

Weight / Mass

Imperial	1 ounce (oz)	1 pound (lb)	2.2 pounds	1 stone	1 ton
Metric	28 g	450 g	1 kg	6.4 kg	1 tonne

Capacity / Volume

Imperial	1 fluid ounce	1 pint	1.75 pints	1 gallon
Metric	30 ml	600 ml	1 litre	4.5 litres

Reading Scales

- When reading scales, first establish what each division stands for:
  - count the gaps (not the lines!) in between the numbers given on the scale
  - subtract the two numbers from each other
  - divide the result by the number of gaps.

Example

What is the reading shown on these weighing scales?

To work out the scale:
- first look at the larger divisions, e.g. 4–5 kg
- subtract the smaller from the larger: 1 kg
- divide this by the number of spaces, making sure you know the units you are using.

So: 1 kg ÷ 5 = 0.2 kg or 1,000 g ÷ 5 = 200 g

The value indicated on the scale is **4.2 kg** or **4 kg 200 g**.

Perimeter and Circumference

- The **perimeter** is the distance around the outside of a 2D shape (like fencing around the edge of a garden).

> **Remember**
>
> Knowing the properties of 2D shapes will help solve perimeter problems.

Example

A regular pentagon has a perimeter of 65 cm. What is the length of one side?

A pentagon has five sides, so to find the length of one side divide the total perimeter by 5.

65 cm ÷ 5 = **13 cm**

- If you are given measurements in different units (such as centimetres and metres), change them so that they are the same before you start your calculations.

Example

Find the perimeter of the shape shown right.

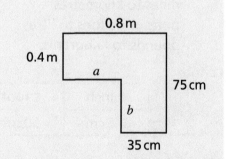

First convert all the measurement to centimetres:

40 cm   80 cm   75 cm   35 cm

Then calculate the measurements of a and b.

To find a: 80 cm − 35 cm = 45 cm
To find b: 75 cm − 40 cm = 35 cm

Now add together all the measurements to find the total perimeter:

40 cm + 80 cm + 75 cm + 35 cm + 35 cm + 45 cm = **310 cm**

- The perimeter of a circle is called the **circumference** (C).
- The circumference can be calculated using the formula:
  $C = \pi \times 2 \times$ radius, or equivalently, $C = \pi \times$ diameter
- The diameter of a circle is twice its radius.

- The value of π (Greek letter 'pi') is slightly more than 3 and it stays the same whatever the size of the circle.

Example

Alison is taking her baby for a walk in a buggy and wants to know how far it is to the park. The back wheel has a circumference of 80 cm. The wheel does 600 revolutions to get to the park. How far away is the park?

80 cm = 0.8 m

$0.8 \times 600 = 8 \times 60 = 48 \times 10 = $ **480 m**

> **Quick Test**
>
> 1. How should the time 4.45 in the afternoon be written?
>   A 14:45   B 16:45   C 18:45   D 04:45   E 15:45
> 2. At the cinema, the adverts and trailers last 25 minutes and the main film lasts 1 hour and 40 minutes, with a five-minute gap in between.
>   If the whole programme starts at 3.20 p.m., what time does it finish?
> 3. At the swimming pool where Simone swims, you pay £3 per hour to use the pool. Simone goes to twelve 40-minute sessions in a month. How much does this cost?
> 4. Emily is weighing ingredients for a cake. The scale currently shows the weight below.
>   She needs to add 800 g dried fruit to the mixture.
>   What will the scale read after she adds it?
>   A 1.48 kg   B 1.804 kg   C 2 kg   D 2.2 kg   E 2.4 kg
> 5. A baby girl drinks 600 ml of milk each day. How many litres of milk does she drink in a week?

Area and Volume

- The area is the surface of a 2D shape.
- Area is measured in units squared, e.g. mm², cm², m².

Rectangle or Square	Parallelogram	Triangle	Circle
Area = Length × Width	Area = Base × Perpendicular height	Area = $\frac{1}{2}$ (Base × Height)	Area = π × Radius²

Rectangle or Square — Width, Length

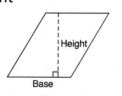
Parallelogram — Height, Base

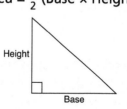
Triangle — Height, Base

Circle — Radius

- You can work out the surface area of a 3D shape by adding together the areas of each individual face.
- 3D shapes have volume (the amount of space inside the shape).
- Volume is measured in units cubed, e.g. mm³, cm³, m³.

Cuboid	Prism or Cylinder
Volume = Length × Width × Height	Volume = Area of cross-section × Length

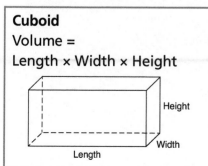
Cuboid — Height, Width, Length

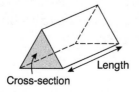
Prism or Cylinder — Length, Cross-section

> **Remember**
>
> The perpendicular height is the shortest distance from the base of the shape to the top; this is **not** the height of a slanted side.

Speed

- Speed is the measure of how distance changes relative to time. If talking about how fast a car travels, we might say it goes at 30 miles per hour (mph). In other words, every hour the car would travel 30 miles.
- At other times speed may be measured metrically in kilometres per hour (kph or km/h) or metres per second (m/s).
- The 'per' means divide. Divide the distance travelled (km) by the time it has taken (hours) to find a speed in kilometres per hour.
- If a speed is known and you want to find the distance, you do the inverse function and multiply by the time taken.
- If you want to find out how long it took to go a certain distance at a set speed, divide the distance travelled by the speed.

Remember

Units need to be consistent. If the speed is measured in kilometres per hour, the time should be in hours and the distance in kilometres. It may be sensible to convert units at the end to make them easier to understand.

Example

A train travels at 50 m/s for 3 minutes. How far does it travel in this time in km?

3 minutes = 3 × 60 = 180 s
50 × 180 = 9,000 m = **9 km**

Example

A cyclist takes two and a half hours to travel 30 miles.
a) Assuming the cyclist went at a constant speed, how fast was she travelling?
    30 ÷ 2.5 = **12 mph**
b) How long would it take her to travel 18 miles at the same speed?
    18 ÷ 12 = 1.5
    It would take **1 hour 30 minutes**.

Remember

Think about what information there is, write things down to keep track of them and draw diagrams if it helps. Sometimes it can help to write down the smaller questions you are going to answer along the way.

Problem Solving

- Problem-solving questions about measure will generally need more than one step to solve.

Example

A builder is tiling a kitchen floor using tiles that are 20 cm by 30 cm. Boxes of tiles cost £32 each and contain 25 tiles. The kitchen floor is a rectangle measuring 2 m by 3.5 m. How much will it cost to buy enough tiles for the kitchen floor?

Answer planning: What is the area of the kitchen floor? (Area of rectangle: $l \times w$)
                    How many m² does each box of tiles cover? (Remember to convert into m)
                    How many boxes are needed? (Divide floor by area from a box, round up)
                    How much will that cost? (Multiply the number of boxes by 32)

Area of kitchen floor = 2 × 3.5 = 7 m²
A tile is 0.2 × 0.3 = 0.06 m²
A box of tiles covers 0.06 × 25 = 1.5 m²
How many boxes? 7 ÷ 1.5 = 4 remainder 1
This means you need more than 4 boxes, so 5 boxes need to be bought.
How much will the tiles cost?   5 × 32 = **£160**

Example

Cara has a long piece of rope. She wraps it around two identical posts that are stuck in the ground, as shown in the diagram. When it has gone around the posts five times, the remaining rope measures 55 cm. How long is the rope?

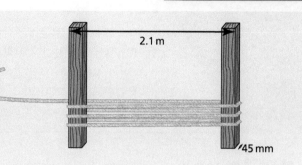

First convert everything into metres:

45 mm = 0.045 m   55 cm = 0.55 m

For one time around the posts:

2.1 + 0.045 + 2.1 + 0.045 = 4.29 m of rope

Five times around the posts = 4.29 × 5

= 42.9 ÷ 2 = 21.45 m

Total length of rope = 21.45 + 0.55 = **22 m**

Quick Test

1. Find:
    a) the volume of this cuboid in cubic centimetres
    b) the surface area in square centimetres.
2. Two of these shapes have the same area. Which are they?

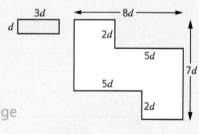

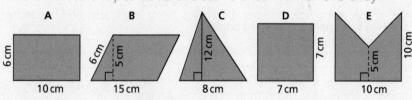

A B and E   B A and B   C C and D   D C and E   E A and C

3. How many copies of the small rectangle would fill up the space inside the large shape?

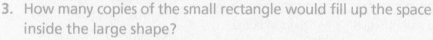

4. There are two routes between Sian's house and her Grandma's. The first route is 14 miles and the average speed for the journey is 28 mph. The second route is 20 miles. If both routes take the same length of time, what is the average speed for the second route?

5. Zak is building a cuboidal pond in his garden for his 15 fish. Each fish needs to have 45 litres of water to avoid overcrowding. 1 m³ = 1,000 litres. The fish also need the water to have a minimum depth of 3 ft (use 1 ft = 30 cm). How many more fish could Zak buy to put in his pond if the depth is the minimum 3 ft?

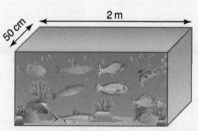

A 0   B 2   C 5   D 10   E 11

Geometry

You should be able to:

- recall and apply the properties of common 2D and 3D shapes
- reflect and rotate shapes
- relate nets to 3D shapes and solve spatial reasoning problems
- solve problems involving angles, including within 2D shapes and in terms of direction or rotation
- work with coordinates and find missing points.

2D Shapes

- 2D shapes are flat and so have just two dimensions (width and length). They can be classified in a number of ways.

Remember

Regular polygons are 2D shapes with equal sides and equal angles.

Shapes with curved sides	Circle		Semi-circle	
	• One side • Infinite lines of symmetry		• Two sides • One line of symmetry	

Shapes with three sides	Equilateral triangle	Right-angled triangle	Isosceles triangle	Scalene triangle
Sides	All equal	Longest side is opposite the right angle	Two equal sides	No equal sides
Angles	All equal (60°)	One right angle	Two base angles are equal	No equal angles
Lines of symmetry	3	1 (if the two sides next to the right angle are of equal length) or 0	1	0

Remember

Other 2D shapes include pentagons (five sides), hexagons (six sides), octagons (eight sides) and decagons (ten sides).

Shapes with four sides (quadrilaterals)	Square	Rectangle	Parallelogram	
Sides	All equal	Two pairs of equal sides	Two pairs of equal sides	
Angles	All equal (90°)	All equal (90°)	Opposite angles are equal	
Lines of symmetry	4	2	0	
Pairs of parallel sides	2	2	2	

More quadrilaterals	Rhombus	Trapezium	Kite
Sides	All equal	No equal sides (but an isosceles trapezium does have one pair of equal sides)	Two pairs of equal sides that are next to each other
Angles	Opposite angles are equal	An isosceles trapezium has two pairs of equal angles	One equal pair of angles
Lines of symmetry	2	1 (if two sides are of equal length) or 0	1
Pairs of parallel sides	2	1	0

3D Shapes

- 3D shapes are solid shapes with three dimensions (width, length and height). They usually have flat faces, straight edges and pointed vertices.
- Two of the most common 3D shapes are:
  - **prisms:** if you imagine slicing prisms like a loaf of bread, the faces remain the same shape and size

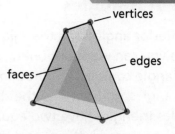

  - **pyramids:** these come to a point at the top, and if you slice them, the face stays the same shape but becomes smaller nearer to the top.

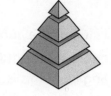

- Note that a hemisphere is a sphere cut in half, so it has one edge and two faces (one curved and one flat).
- The properties of some common 3D shapes are:

3D shape	Sphere	Cylinder	Cube	Cuboid	Triangular prism	Tetrahedron (triangular-based pyramid)	Square-based pyramid
Edges	0	2	12	12	9	6	8
Vertices	0	0	8	8	6	4	5
Faces	1	3	6	6	5	4	5

Types of Angle

- Angles are created when two straight lines meet or intersect.
- Angles on a straight line sum to 180°.
- Angles at a point sum to 360°.

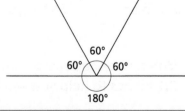

Acute angle	Right angle	Obtuse angle	Reflex angle
Makes less than a quarter turn (90°).	Makes a quarter turn (90°).	Makes more than a quarter turn (90°) but less than a half turn (180°).	Makes more than a half turn (180°).

Unknown Angles in Shapes

Angles in Triangles

- The interior angles of a triangle always add up to 180°. This means you can work out unknown angles.
- If a triangle contains a right angle and you know one of the other angles, you can find the third angle.
- Isosceles triangles have two equal sides (often marked with a single line through them) and therefore two equal angles.

Example

Work out the value of the angle x.

Angles in a triangle sum to 180°.
The two base angles of this isosceles triangle both equal 43°.
$43° \times 2 = 86°$
So $x = 180 - 86 =$ **94°**

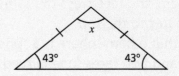

Angles in Quadrilaterals

- The interior angles of a quadrilateral always add up to 360°.
- Particular types of quadrilateral have extra properties:
  - Squares and rectangles have four equal angles of 90°.
  - Parallelograms and rhombuses have two pairs of opposite angles that are equal.
- If you know any of the angles in a parallelogram, you can work out the other three.
- Kites have two opposite angles that are equal.

Example

In this kite, angle a is 90° and angle b is 100°.

Work out the values of angles c and d.

Angle c must be the same as b, so $c =$ **100°**
And therefore $d = 360 - (90 + 100 + 100) =$ **70°**

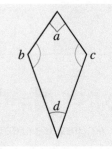

- When two shapes are joined together, use your knowledge of 2D shapes to help you work out the angles.

Example

If angle $a = 52°$ and angle $b = 43°$, work out all of the other angles.

Because angles a, b and c form a triangle: $c = 180° - (43° + 52°) =$ **85°**

We know $c + d = 180°$ (point on a straight line) so: $d = 180° - 85° =$ **95°**

As angles d, e, f, g form a rhombus, $f = d$, so: $e + g = 360° - (95° + 95°) = 170°$

Angles e and g are also equal so: $e = g = 170° \div 2 =$ **85°**

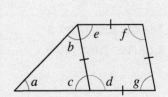

Symmetry, Reflection and Rotation

- A line of symmetry is often represented by a dashed line.
- In the lettering shown (right), A, C, D and T all have one line of symmetry. F has no lines of symmetry and O and H have two lines of symmetry. If the O was written as a perfect circle, it would have an infinite number of symmetry lines.
- Reflection is where a shape is formed using a line of symmetry as the 'mirror line'.

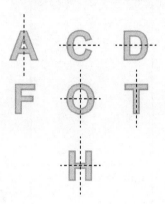

Example

Reflect each shape in the dashed line:

Diagonal lines tend to be a bit trickier to see how the shape will behave.

- **Rotational symmetry** is where the object can be placed in different positions, by rotating it, but still appear the same.

Example

There are five different ways this regular pentagon could fit back into the jigsaw space. A regular pentagon has rotational symmetry of order 5. (Note: the smiley face icon is used to show how the shape is being rotated).

Nets and 3D Spatial Reasoning

- A net is an 'unfolded' shape. A net can be folded in different ways to make a 3D shape.

Remember

You can think of rotational symmetry like a child's wooden jigsaw where the shape could fit in the hole in different ways. The order of rotational symmetry is how many ways the piece would fit back into the space as it was turned through 360°.

Remember

All of the shapes in a net form the faces of the shape. The net of a cube will be made of six identical squares.

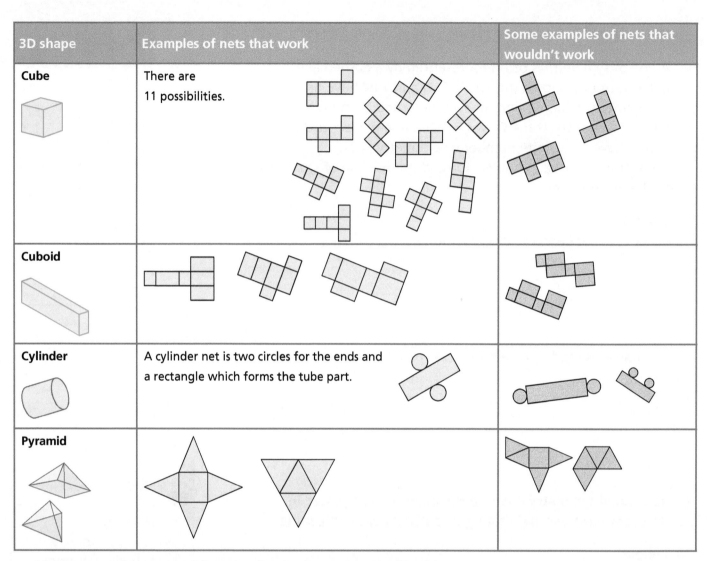

3D shape	Examples of nets that work	Some examples of nets that wouldn't work
Cube	There are 11 possibilities.	
Cuboid		
Cylinder	A cylinder net is two circles for the ends and a rectangle which forms the tube part.	
Pyramid		

- You may need to use your imagination to move around a 3D object and think about what it would look like from different sides.

Example
Toby makes the building (shown right) out of toy blocks.
The image shows the front of his building.
Which picture shows the back of Toby's building?

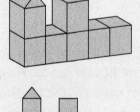

A   B   C   D

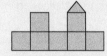 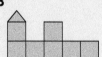 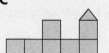

Imagine that you are standing behind the blocks and looking at them from that side. What would you see? The answer is **C**.

Compass Directions

- A compass is split into four main directions: North (N), South (S), East (E) and West (W).
- From any point, you can use a compass to define which way you are facing. If you face North and then turn 90° to your right (clockwise), you will be facing East. Turn another 90° to the right and you will be facing South, and so on.

- Make sure you know the intermediate directions of North-East (NE), South-East (SE), South-West (SW) and North-West (NW).
- When facing North, a turn of 45° anti-clockwise turns you to NW.

Example

Carla is facing North-West and then turns anti-clockwise through 135°. Which compass direction is she facing now?

Drawing the compass points can be helpful. 135° = 90° + 45°

From NW, turning 135° anti-clockwise will take her to **South**.

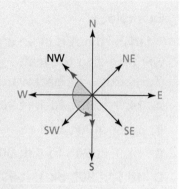

Coordinate Grids

- Using the scales on the two axes of a grid helps to locate points. Simple coordinates are shown on a positive grid:
  - There are two axes, x (horizontal) and y (vertical).
  - The x coordinate is always written before the y coordinate in the form (x, y).
- More complex coordinates are shown on grids arranged in four quadrants which include negative numbers.

> **Remember**
>
> The order in which you should read coordinates can be remembered by a plane taking off – it has to travel horizontally (x) down the runway before gaining (vertical) height (y).

Example

Triangle ABC is an isosceles triangle. If the coordinates for A are (3, 12) and the coordinates for C are (–3, –6), find the coordinates of B.

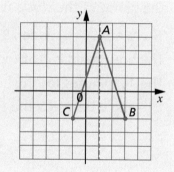

Draw in the line of symmetry for the isosceles triangle.
Mark the scale onto the y- and x-axis: each interval equals 3.
x-axis coordinate, four intervals between C and B: $-3 + (4 \times 3) = 9$
y-axis coordinate, six intervals between A and B: $12 - (6 \times 3) = -6$
The coordinates of B are **(9, –6)**.

Translating 2D Shapes

- Translation moves a 2D shape into a new position on a grid using given directions.
- The shape stays exactly the same and is not rotated or reflected.

Example

The triangle ABC is translated by four squares to the left and two squares down. Find the new coordinates of C.

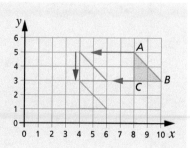

Mark vertex C with a dot. Count four squares left and then two squares down using the dot as a marker.

The new coordinates of C are **(4, 1)**.

Problem Solving

- You will need to understand different types of direction to work out puzzles involving maps or moving objects through a maze.

> **Remember**
>
> Think about which direction the object is facing after each movement.

Example

A ladybird bot is in an enclosed maze. Find which instruction set will take it to the leaf.
(forwards = fd, backwards = bk, right = rt, left = lt)

A bk 1, lt 90°, fd 1, rt 90°, fd 3

B fd 5, rt 90°, fd 1

C bk 1, rt 90°, fd 4, lt 90°, fd 1

D fd 5, lt 90°, bk 1, lt 90°, fd 2, lt 90°, fd 2

E fd 3, rt 270°, fd 1, rt 90°, fd 2

Option **E** will take it to the leaf.

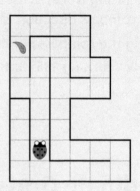

- A clock face is split into 12 equal sectors; each one is a 30° turn. The minute hand moves 30° every five minutes.
- To find the angles between clock hands, remember that the hour hand moves constantly too. Every hour that passes, the hour hand moves 30° around the clock face.

> **Remember**
>
> In 15 minutes, the minute hand will turn 90°.

Example

A clock shows the time is ten to twelve. What is the size of the angle made by the hands of the clock at this time?

There are 90° between 9 and 12. So each step, say between 10 and 11, is 30°.

The hour hand is $\frac{5}{6}$ of the way between 11 and 12.

The 10 minutes for the hour hand is $\frac{1}{6}$ of 30° = 5°.

The angle between the two hands is 30° + 25° = **55°**.

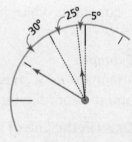

> **Quick Test**

1. How many lines of symmetry does a regular pentagon have?
2. Shown on the right is a net diagram of a cube. How many edges of the cube appear twice in the net diagram?
   A 4   B 5   C 6   D 7   E 8
3. The diagram (far right) shows a kite. Find the size of the angle marked x.
4. A fourth point D is added to the diagram (below right) so that ABCD form a square. What are the coordinates of D?
5. The end points of five lines are given below. Which pair of points forms a line parallel to the one shown in the diagram (right)?
   A (−2, 1) and (2, −1)
   B (−5, 1) and (4, 4)
   C (−4, 0) and (2, 3)
   D (−2, 0) and (3, 0)
   E (2, 2) and (5, 3)

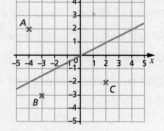

Statistics

You should be able to:
- read information from a range of statistical charts and graphs
- use the information given to find missing values or carry out calculations
- work out the average from a set of data.

Two-way Tables

- A two-way table shows information that relates to two different categories. You should be able to understand the information shown and be able to work out any missing values.

Example

Ashish's mum is placing an order for his school photo. There are four different photo packs available and she has started completing the order form:

	Price	Quantity	Total
Pack 1	£6.00		
Pack 2	£8.50	0	£0
Pack 3	£13.50	1	£13.50
Pack 4	£18.50	1	£18.50
		Postage	£1.75
		Total	£51.75

Ashish's mum still needs to fill in the row for Pack 1 but she will spend a total of £51.75, including £1.75 postage. How many lots of Pack 1 is Ashish's mum ordering?

First work out the cost of the packs ordered so far, plus the postage:

£13.50 + £18.50 + £1.75 = £33.75

Subtract this cost from the total: £51.75 − £33.75 = £18.00

The cost of each Pack 1 ordered is £6.00, so: £18.00 ÷ 6 = 3

She must be ordering **3** lots of Pack 1.

Distance Charts

- These charts show the distance between any places on the chart. To find a distance, read down from one place and across to the other.

Example

Look at this distance chart. How far is it from Longwell to Streetbridge?

Teeford				
390 km	Longwell			
245 km	296 km	Redham		
147 km	140 km	170 km	Streetbridge	
331 km	121 km	113 km	31 km	Octon

Follow the Longwell column down until you reach the Streetbridge row. The answer is **140 km**.

Pictograms

- Pictograms use small pictures or symbols to show amounts.
- Make sure you check what each small picture or symbol represents.

Example

This pictogram shows the number of children from classes who chose different fruit for their snack on Tuesday.
How many children were there altogether?

Multiply the whole fruits by the number they represent, then work out the proportions of the fractions to complete the calculations for each row.

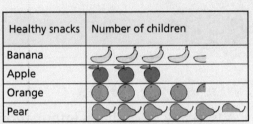

Healthy snacks	Number of children
Banana	
Apple	
Orange	
Pear	

Each full fruit symbol represents eight children

Bananas: $(4 \times 8) + (\frac{1}{2} \times 8) = 32 + 4 = 36$

Apples: $3 \times 8 = 24$

Oranges: $(4 \times 8) + (\frac{1}{4} \times 8) = 32 + 2 = 34$

Pears: $(5 \times 8) + (\frac{1}{2} \times 8) = 40 + 4 = 44$

Add up the totals: $36 + 24 + 34 + 44 = $ **138** children altogether

Bar Charts

- Bar charts compare frequencies (how many of one thing there are compared to another).

Example

Look at this bar chart, which shows how a class of pupils travel to school.
How many more children travel to school by car than by bicycle?

Read the values on the bar chart:
15 pupils travel by car and 5 pupils by bicycle.

So $15 - 5 = $ **10** more pupils travel to school by car than by bicycle.

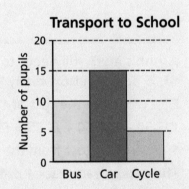

Transport to School

Line Graphs

- Line graphs can represent two different types of information: time-based data and conversion data.
- Time-based graphs show what happens to a measurement over time. It is important to check the time units when answering questions.
- The steepness of the line graph represents the rate of the change; a steep line shows a greater rate of change than a less steep line.

Example

Look at this line graph showing hours of sunshine in a village over the course of one week. How many days had 7 hours or more of sunshine?

For each day of the week, read straight up from the horizontal axis until you reach the line. Then read across to find the number of hours of sunshine for that day:

Monday: 5 hours of sunshine; Tuesday: 6 hours; Wednesday: 5 hours; Thursday: 7 hours; Friday: 8 hours; Saturday: 8 hours; Sunday: 6 hours

So **three** days of the week (Thursday, Friday and Saturday) had 7 hours or more of sunshine.

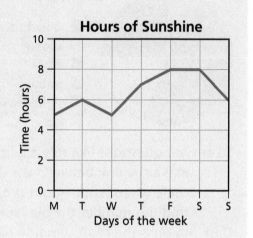

- Conversion graphs show relationships between amounts and how they compare in proportion. It is important to check the scale on both the x-axis and the y-axis.

Example

Look at the conversion graph.
How many euros would you get for £15?

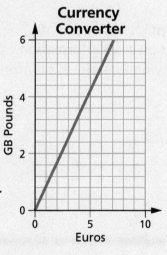

The vertical axis doesn't reach as far as £15, but the constant steepness of the line shows that the rate of change is the same for all values.

If we find out how many euros £5 would be worth, we can multiply that value by 3 to get the conversion for £15.

From the vertical axis, read straight across until you reach the line of the graph. At that point, read directly down to find the equivalent value in euros.

The graph shows that £5 is equivalent to 6 euros.

6 × 3 = 18, so £15 is worth **18** euros.

Remember

Harder questions may show line graphs which are curved rather than straight and/or they may ask you to find the difference between two points on the line.

Pie Charts

- Pie charts are used to show fractions of a whole.
- The size of each segment of the circle represents the fraction of the whole.

Example

The pie chart below shows the hair colour of a group of parents. There are 16 parents in the group.

How many parents have the most common hair colour?

Hair Colour

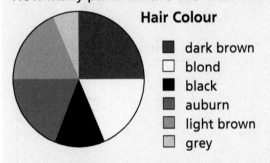

- ■ dark brown
- □ blond
- ■ black
- ■ auburn
- ■ light brown
- □ grey

To answer questions like this it is important to:
- – make the link between the degrees at the centre of a circle when working out proportions
- – find the number the pie represents.

Dark brown is the most common hair colour in this group and the dark brown segment represents $\frac{1}{4}$ of the parents. If there are 16 parents in total, then **four** of them have dark brown hair.

Venn Diagrams

- Venn diagrams show the relationships between data.
- Each circle represents a particular piece of information.
- Overlapping circles show where two more pieces of information share a common feature.

Example

Look at the Venn diagram shown (right).

Find the shape that fits into the section labelled 'x' in the diagram.

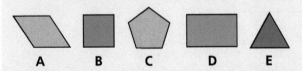

A B C D E

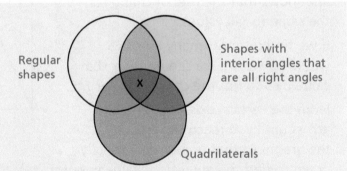

Regular shapes

Shapes with interior angles that are all right angles

Quadrilaterals

The answer is **B** because it is the only shape that shares all three properties: it is a regular quadrilateral with interior angles that are right angles.

Sorting Diagrams

- Sorting diagrams are used to sort objects or numbers into a grid – similar to a two-way table – depending on their properties.

Example

Look at this sorting diagram for numbers up to 30. It is not fully completed.

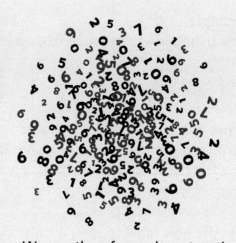

	Even numbers	Odd numbers
Prime numbers	2	3 5 7 11 13 17 19 23 29
Square numbers	?	1 9 25

Find a number which could be placed in the part of the diagram marked '?'

A 27   **B** 10   **C** 12   **D** 16   **E** 28

The answer must be both an even number and a square number. We can therefore rule out option A straight away, since it is an odd number. All the other options are even numbers but only one is a square number, i.e. 16. So the correct answer is **D**.

Average (Mean)

- The average, or the mean, is the sum of all the values divided by the number of values.
- So the mean of the numbers 2, 4, 4, 4, 5, 5, 6, 7, 8 is:

$$\frac{2 + 4 + 4 + 4 + 5 + 5 + 6 + 7 + 8}{9} = \frac{45}{9} = 5$$

> **Remember**
>
> The mean can also be a fraction. If the number of children in five houses is 0, 1, 2, 2, 3, then the mean number of children per house is: $\frac{0 + 1 + 2 + 2 + 3}{5} = 1.6$ (even though you cannot have 0.6 of a child for real!)

Example

Romesh bought some apples while shopping at a supermarket. He bought two packs of six apples which each cost £1.20. He also bought three single apples which cost 30p each. What was the average cost of each apple that Romesh bought?

First work out how many apples Romesh bought and how much he spent in total on them:

He bought two packs of six and three single apples, so 6 + 6 + 3 = 15 apples in total

Two packs at a price of £1.20 each: 2 × £1.20 = £2.40

Three single apples at a price of 30p each: 3 × £0.30 = £0.90

Total spent on apples: £2.40 + £0.90 = £3.30 (or 330p)

To work out the average cost, divide the total cost by the number of apples bought:

330 ÷ 15 = **22p** per apple

Averages from Frequency Tables

- Frequency tables often cause confusion. You need to remember that the frequency tells you how many numbers or data items there are altogether.

Example
This table shows the results of a survey of shoe sizes among children at a tennis club:

Shoe size	1	2	3	4	5
Frequency	2	1	6	1	2

What is the average shoe size among these children?
Write out the frequency line again, splitting this into the number of children with each shoe size.
The frequency total is 12, so there are 12 children.

Frequency	1, 1	2	3, 3, 3, 3, 3, 3	4	5, 5

Use the new table to work out the mean:

$1 + 1 + 2 + 3 + 3 + 3 + 3 + 3 + 3 + 4 + 5 + 5 = 36$

$36 \div 12 = 3$

The average shoe size is **3**.

Quick Test

1. The pictogram shows the results of a survey of favourite arts subjects among a group of pupils. How many more pupils prefer art compared with drama?

Favourite Arts Subject

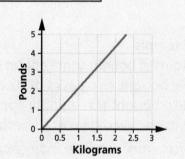

2. The line graph, shown far right, converts kilograms to pounds.
   How many pounds is 1.5 kg?
   A 0.6   B 0.7   C 1.1   D 2.2   E 3.3

3. This pie chart shows the percentages of different kinds of jam sold in a supermarket in one week.
   If the supermarket sold 45 jars of blackcurrant jam, how many jars of strawberry jam were sold?

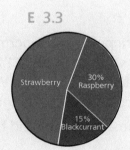
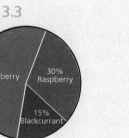

4. The table below shows the number of merit points scored in a class during the 12 weeks of term. The number of merit points for week 12 is missing.

Week	1	2	3	4	5	6	7	8	9	10	11	12
Merit points	6	5	6	8	10	7	6	7	10	3	10	?

If the mean number of merit points across the whole term was 7, how many merit points were scored in week 12?

Collins

11+
Maths

Practice

Workbook

YOU HAVE 54 QUESTIONS TO COMPLETE WITHIN THE TIME GIVEN.

Mark the Digits

The questions within this section are not multiple choice. Write the answer to each question on the answer sheet by selecting the correct digits from the columns provided.

Example i

Calculate the answer to the following:

12 + 42

The correct answer is **54**. This has already been marked in Example i for Practice Test 1 on your answer sheet on page 155.

Example ii

Calculate the answer to the following:

55 – 47

The correct answer is **8**. Mark this in Example ii for Practice Test 1 on your answer sheet on page 155.

Note that a single-digit answer should be marked with a 0 in the left-hand column, so mark 08 on your answer sheet.

1. Calculate the answer to the following:

   17 + 56

2. Calculate the answer to the following:

   120 ÷ 2

3. Calculate the answer to the following:

   54 − 7 + 9

4. What is the mean of these numbers?

   12, 18, 10, 4

5. Which number should replace the '?' in the following sequence?

   14, 21, 29, 36, ?, 51

6. How many minutes are there in $1\frac{1}{6}$ hours?

7. What is the value of X in this equation?

   $15 + X = 31 - 12$

8. What is the remainder when 75 is divided by 8?

9. How many months are there in half a decade?

10. Which of these is not a multiple of 8?

    40, 65, 88, 24, 56

11. How many different factors does the number 36 have?

12. I think of a number, multiply it by 2 and then divide it by 3. My answer is 8.

    What number did I think of?

13. Calculate the answer to the following:

    74 − 59

14. Which number comes next in the following sequence?

    17, 24, 30, 35, 39, ?

15 Which of these numbers is not divisible by 3?

18, 15, 12, 33, 48, 27, 55

16 How many quarters are there in $8\frac{3}{4}$?

17 Calculate the value of X in the equation below.

$0.5 = \frac{8}{X}$

18 What is the remainder when 55 is divided by 11?

19 How many millimetres are there in 4.8 cm?

20 How much greater is $\frac{1}{4}$ of 60 than $\frac{1}{5}$ of 70?

21 Calculate the mean of the following numbers:

8, 4, 7, 9, 2

22 How many weeks are there in half a year?

23 Omar runs at a speed of 10 kilometres per hour.

How many minutes will it take Omar to run 2.5 km?

24 Calculate the answer to the following:

$7 + (6 \times 9) - 3$

25 What is $\frac{1}{4}$ of 256?

26 Which number should replace the '?' in the following sequence?

12, 14, 11, ?, 10, 12, 9

27 What is the perimeter of this equilateral triangle in centimetres?

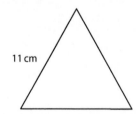

11 cm

28 Last year, Bob was 7 years old.

How old will Bob be in three years' time?

29 There are 7 Kags in 1 Kog. There are 8 Kogs in 1 Kig.

How many Kags are there in 1 Kig?

30 How many more edges than faces does a cube have?

31 Subtract four hundred and ninety-one from five hundred and seventy-nine.

32 Kelly eats three meals per day.

How many meals does Kelly eat in a fortnight?

33 A jug contains $\frac{3}{4}$ of a litre of water. A cup has a capacity of 75 ml.

How many identical cups can be filled with the water in the jug?

34 Tara showers once per day from 27th September to 2nd October, inclusive.

How many times does Tara shower in this period?

35 A plastic button weighs 40 g. The total weight of identical plastic buttons in a basket is 0.8 kg.

How many plastic buttons are in the basket?

36 How much greater is $\frac{1}{4}$ of 44 than $\frac{1}{3}$ of 33?

37 Calculate the answer to the following:

123 – 24

38 Calculate the value of X in the following equation:

$4X - 3 = 45$

39 Calculate the next term in the following sequence:

45, 37, 29, 21, ?

40 What number is 6 less than double 36?

41 What is the area of this rectangle in cm²?

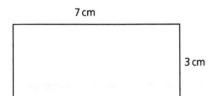

7 cm

3 cm

42 What is the total number of days in the last two months of the year?

43 Calculate the mean of the following data:

5, 7, 23, 12, 5, 14

44 Calculate the answer to the following:

−10 + 20

45 The cost of renting a car is £210 per day. Emily and two friends rent the car for one day. They split the cost equally between them.

How much do they each pay in pounds?

46 The ratio 3 : 9 is equal to the ratio D : 45

What is the value of D?

47 How many different factors does the number 24 have?

48 A bookseller decides to raise the price of a £5 book by 40%.

What is the new price of the book in pounds?

49 The perimeter of an octagon is 46.3 cm. All but one of its sides each have a length of 5.9 cm.

What is the length in centimetres of the remaining side of the octagon?

50 What is the smallest number of coins from which I could make £0.78 exactly?

51 How many sevenths of an orange are there in four whole oranges?

52 Five children each receive three pencils and four books.

How many books do they receive in total?

53 Tom is third from the front of a queue and third from the back.

How many people are there in the queue?

54 Calculate the answer to the following:

$\frac{1}{4}$ of $\frac{1}{2}$ of 88

END OF TEST

YOU HAVE 53 QUESTIONS TO COMPLETE WITHIN THE TIME GIVEN.

Mark the Digits

The questions within this section are not multiple choice. Write the answer to each question on the answer sheet by selecting the correct digits from the columns provided.

Example i

Calculate the answer to the following:

12 + 42

The correct answer is **54**. This has already been marked in Example i for Practice Test 2 on your answer sheet on page 157.

Example ii

Calculate the answer to the following:

55 – 47

The correct answer is **8**. Mark this in Example ii for Practice Test 2 on your answer sheet on page 157.

Note that a single-digit answer should be marked with a 0 in the left-hand column, so mark 08 on your answer sheet.

1. Calculate the answer to the following:

   $123 + 456$

2. Calculate the answer to the following:

   $477 \div 3$

3. Calculate the answer to the following:

   $32 + 64 + 19 - 12$

4. Which number should replace the ? in the following sequence?

   74, 71, 66, 63, ?, 55

5. Calculate the mean of the following numbers:

   14, 12, 5, 6, 18

6. How many hours are there in three whole days?

7. What is the value of Y in this equation?

   $11 + 2Y = 44 - 13$

8. David watched television from 8.30 a.m. until 11.15 a.m.

   For how many minutes did David watch television?

9. How many more factors does the number 48 have than the number 10?

10. A van can hold 40 boxes. Each box can hold 24 bananas.

    How many bananas can the van hold?

11. How many squares with a side length of 4 cm can fit on a rectangular board that measures 8 cm by 12 cm?

12. $\frac{1}{3}$ of X is 32. What is $\frac{1}{2}$ of X?

13. There were 30 birds in a tree on Tuesday. On Wednesday, the number of birds in the tree increased by 30%.

    How many birds were in the tree on Wednesday?

14 Calculate the answer to the following:

$(642 \div 2) \div 3$

15 Which number comes next in the following sequence?

1, 4, 9, 16, 25, ?

16 What is the numerator when $\frac{1}{2}$ is added to $\frac{1}{6}$ and expressed in its lowest terms?

17 Calculate the value of X in the following equation:

$0.4 = \frac{X}{20}$

18 How many tenths greater is 4.567 rounded to 1 decimal place than 4.291 rounded to 1 decimal place?

19 Calculate the value of X in the following equation:

$7X - 7 = 2X + 28$

20 I think of a number, divide it by 3, multiply it by 4 and then add 1. My answer is 49.

What number did I think of?

21 Calculate $\frac{7}{5}$ of 80.

22 What is $\frac{1}{4}$ of $\frac{1}{2}$ of 96?

23 How many weeks are there in two years?

24 A square plate has sides of 4 cm.

How many square plates can fit side by side on a square piece of paper which has sides of 16 cm?

25 How many vertices does a cube have?

26 A water tank can hold a maximum of 65 litres of water.

If the water tank is $\frac{3}{5}$ full, how many more litres of water could it hold?

27 A plant grows 3 cm per day. If the plant measures 12 cm at the beginning of 30th July, what will its height be in centimetres at the end of 3rd August?

28 What number should come next in the following sequence?

43, 45, 49, 57, ?

29 How many lines of symmetry does this isosceles triangle have?

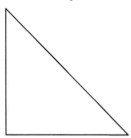

30 Calculate the answer to the following:
6,850 – 5,874

31 How many more fifths are there in 10 than thirds in 8?

32 Calculate the answer to the following:

74 – (8 + 16)

33 A car travels at 120 kilometres per hour.

How many kilometres will the car have covered in $\frac{1}{6}$ of an hour?

34 How many millimetres are there in 1 metre?

35 Subtract eighty-nine from three thousand and twenty-seven.

36 Gina walks her dog twice per day. Each walk is 2.5 km.

What distance, in kilometres, does Gina walk with her dog in the month of November?

37 Calculate the answer to the following:

264 – 219

38 Calculate the value of X in the following equation:

$3X + 7 = 2(X + 4)$

39 Calculate the next number in the following sequence:

23, 19, 14, 10, 5, ?

40 I think of a number, add 4 to it, divide by 2 and then multiply by 3. My answer is 30.

What number did I think of?

41 How many more days are there in July and August combined than in October and November combined?

42 Bruno, Monty and Joey are three different breeds of dog. Bruno is twice as tall as Monty. Monty is three times as tall as Joey.

If Joey is 15 cm tall, how tall is Bruno in cm?

43 A worker can complete 7 tasks per minute.

How many tasks can 7 workers complete in 7 minutes?

44 Two years ago, I was 11 years old. How old will I be in three years' time?

45 How many lines of symmetry does this shape have?

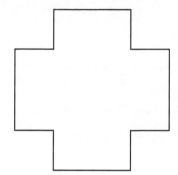

46 A dog's walking speed is measured at 100 metres per minute.

What is the dog's walking speed in kilometres per hour?

47 I eat $\frac{5}{7}$ of the sweets in a bag. 14 sweets remain in the bag.

How many sweets did I eat?

48 Ajit and Rom take a test with 50 questions, each worth 1 mark. Ajit scores 60% of the total marks available.

Rom gets 10% more than Ajit's score.

How many marks did Rom score?

49 There are 52 cards in a deck. I remove $\frac{1}{4}$ of them and then select $\frac{2}{3}$ of the remainder.

How many cards do I select?

50 How many sevenths are there in $6\frac{2}{7}$?

51 Caps cost £2.50 and belts cost £4.50. How many caps can I buy with £24.50?

52 For the month of August, the sun shone for an average of $\frac{1}{3}$ of each day.

On average, for how many hours did the sun shine each day?

53 Calculate the answer to the following:

9,898 – 8,989

END OF TEST

YOU HAVE 30 QUESTIONS TO COMPLETE WITHIN THE TIME GIVEN.

Multiple Choice

The questions within this section are multiple choice. Write the answer to each question on the answer sheet by selecting A, B, C, D or E.

Example i

Calculate the answer to the following:

Tom buys a chocolate bar for £1.50. He pays with a £5 note.

How much change does he receive?

A	B	C	D	E
£1.50	£3	£3.50	£4	£5

The correct answer is **C**. This has already been marked in Example i for Practice Test 3 on your answer sheet on page 159.

Example ii

Sarah eats $\frac{1}{4}$ of a pizza. What fraction of the pizza remains?

A	B	C	D	E
$\frac{1}{2}$	$\frac{1}{3}$	$\frac{2}{5}$	$\frac{3}{4}$	$\frac{5}{6}$

The correct answer is **D**. Mark this in Example ii for Practice Test 3 on your answer sheet on page 159.

Calculate the answers to the following.

1 Peter leaves home at 10 a.m. and returns at 12.30 p.m. For how many minutes is Peter away from home?

A	B	C	D	E
120 minutes	90 minutes	180 minutes	100 minutes	150 minutes

2 A man drives a truck at an average speed of 48 kilometres per hour. What distance does the man cover if he drives for 3 hours?

A	B	C	D	E
148 km	96 km	144 km	100 km	150 km

3 Sandra collects coins. In June, she collected 45 coins. In July, she collected 66 coins. In August, she collected 34 coins. How many coins did she collect in total in June, July and August?

A	B	C	D	E
79	145	48	142	100

4 There are 44 sweets in a box. Ravi eats one quarter of them. How many sweets are left in the box?

A	B	C	D	E
44	0	22	11	33

5 Simon buys two packets of crisps. Each packet costs 22p. He pays with a £1 coin. How much change does Simon receive?

A	B	C	D	E
£0.22	£0.44	£0.78	£0.56	£0.88

6 Shape A is a regular hexagon with a perimeter of 54 cm.
What is the length of one side of Shape A?

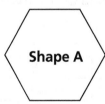

Shape A

A	B	C	D	E
54 cm	12 cm	9 cm	6 cm	27 cm

7 A bowl of sweets is shared between Tim and Robert using a ratio of 3 : 2. If Robert receives 12 sweets, how many does Tim receive?

A	B	C	D	E
18	12	5	6	8

8 How many lines of symmetry does this shape have?

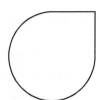

A	B	C	D	E
0	1	2	3	4

9 560 people attended a concert, rounded to the nearest 10. What is the largest possible number of people that could have attended the concert?

A	B	C	D	E
560	550	565	555	564

10 The price of a dress is reduced by 20% in a sale. If the original price was £40, what is the sale price?

A	B	C	D	E
£40	£36	£24	£32	£8

11 Linda has 7 red balls, 6 green balls, 5 yellow balls and 2 black balls. What fraction of Linda's balls are not green?

A	B	C	D	E
$\frac{6}{20}$	$\frac{7}{10}$	$\frac{3}{5}$	$\frac{13}{20}$	$\frac{1}{2}$

12 A circle has a radius of 32 cm. What is the diameter of the circle?

A	B	C	D	E
8 cm	16 cm	32 cm	64 cm	72 cm

13 Calculate the mean of the following numbers:

22, 18, 23, 33

A	B	C	D	E
25	26	28	22	24

14 What is the sum of the three smallest positive prime numbers?

A	B	C	D	E
0	1	6	9	10

15 I roll a fair, six-sided dice. What is the probability that I roll an even number?

A	B	C	D	E
$\frac{5}{6}$	$\frac{1}{2}$	$\frac{1}{3}$	$\frac{2}{3}$	$\frac{1}{6}$

16 The coordinates of three vertices of a square are (2, 2), (2, 6) and (6, 2). What are the coordinates of the fourth vertex of the square?

A	B	C	D	E
(6, 6)	(2, 4)	(6, 4)	(4, 2)	(3, 6)

17 Calculate the answer to the following: $\frac{1}{2} + \frac{1}{3}$

A	B	C	D	E
$\frac{1}{2}$	$\frac{7}{8}$	$\frac{2}{5}$	$\frac{5}{6}$	$\frac{1}{5}$

18 Calculate the answer to the following: $\frac{2}{3} \times \frac{1}{4}$

A	B	C	D	E
$\frac{3}{12}$	$\frac{2}{7}$	$\frac{1}{6}$	$\frac{1}{3}$	$\frac{1}{2}$

19 Calculate the answer to the following: $\frac{1}{2} \div 3$

A	B	C	D	E
$\frac{1}{4}$	$\frac{1}{3}$	$\frac{1}{5}$	$\frac{3}{8}$	$\frac{1}{6}$

20 The number D is three times larger than the number P.

The number F is twice as large as the number D.

Which expression shows the value of the number F in terms of P?

A	B	C	D	E
$0P$	$2P$	$3P$	$\frac{P}{2}$	$6P$

21 The length of a rectangle is twice its width. If the rectangle has a length of 7 cm, what is the perimeter of the rectangle?

A	B	C	D	E
7 cm	14 cm	3.5 cm	28 cm	21 cm

22 A clock shows a time of 12.22 p.m. The clock is 35 minutes fast. What is the correct time?

A	B	C	D	E
12.57 p.m.	11.22 a.m.	11.45 p.m.	11.47 a.m.	12.45 p.m.

23 What is the value of X in the equation below?

$4X + 3X = 54 - 2X$

A	B	C	D	E
9	8	7	6	5

24 A ten-pence coin has a weight of 7 grams. Gill has £1 worth of ten-pence coins. What is the total weight of Gill's coins?

A	B	C	D	E
7 g	14 g	20 g	35 g	70 g

25 A cat drinks a litre of water every 3 days. How many days will 18 litres of water last it?

A	B	C	D	E
18 days	6 days	26 days	54 days	48 days

26 Ken takes a test and gets 4 out of every 5 questions correct. What percentage of the questions does Ken get correct?

A	B	C	D	E
40%	20%	80%	90%	75%

27 Henry has a piece of string that measures 1.5 metres. He cuts the piece of string into 10 equal parts. What is the total length of three of the parts?

A	B	C	D	E
20 cm	50 cm	90 cm	30 cm	45 cm

28 Hannah is facing in a north-west direction. She turns 180° clockwise. What direction is Hannah now facing?

A	B	C	D	E
north-east	south-west	west	south-east	east

29 What is the value of B on the number line here?

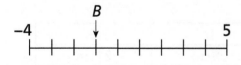

A	B	C	D	E
−3	0	2.5	−1	4

30 10 men take 3 hours to build a fence. How long would it take 20 men to build the same fence?

A	B	C	D	E
3 hours	6 hours	2 hours	1.5 hours	1 hour

END OF TEST

YOU HAVE 30 QUESTIONS TO COMPLETE WITHIN THE TIME GIVEN.

Multiple Choice

The questions within this section are multiple choice. Write the answer to each question on the answer sheet by selecting A, B, C, D or E.

Example i

Calculate the answer to the following:

Tom buys a chocolate bar for £1.50. He pays with a £5 note.

How much change does he receive?

A	B	C	D	E
£1.50	£3	£3.50	£4	£5

The correct answer is **C**. This has already been marked in Example i for Practice Test 4 on your answer sheet on page 159.

Example ii

Sarah eats $\frac{1}{4}$ of a pizza. What fraction of the pizza remains?

A	B	C	D	E
$\frac{1}{2}$	$\frac{1}{3}$	$\frac{2}{5}$	$\frac{3}{4}$	$\frac{5}{6}$

The correct answer is **D**. Mark this in Example ii for Practice Test 4 on your answer sheet on page 159.

Calculate the answers to the following.

1 Zac and his friends watch a film. The film is 1 hour 35 minutes long. If they start watching the film at 7.50 p.m., what will the time be when the film ends?

A	B	C	D	E
7.35 p.m.	9.25 p.m.	8.50 p.m.	7.50 a.m.	9.15 p.m.

2 What is this shape called?

A	B	C	D	E
decagon	pentagon	octagon	hexagon	quadrilateral

3 What is 20^2?

A	B	C	D	E
20	40	400	800	80

4 Ella orders a pizza and eats $\frac{1}{3}$ of it. She then gives $\frac{1}{2}$ of the remainder to her brother. What fraction of the whole pizza does Ella give to her brother?

A	B	C	D	E
$\frac{1}{2}$	$\frac{1}{3}$	$\frac{1}{4}$	$\frac{2}{3}$	$\frac{5}{6}$

5 Ben, Harry and Mia win a lottery prize of £30,000. They share it in the ratio $3:1:2$. How much money does Mia receive?

A	B	C	D	E
£1,000	£5,000	£10,000	£20,000	£30,000

6 A white triangle has a base of 18 cm and a height of 10 cm. Lora shades $\frac{1}{3}$ of the triangle black. What area of the triangle is now shaded black?

A	B	C	D	E
180 cm²	30 cm²	10 cm²	60 cm²	90 cm²

7 1 out of every 8 attendees at a conference has ginger hair. 3 out of every 4 attendees at the conference have black hair. What fraction of the conference attendees has neither ginger nor black hair?

A	B	C	D	E
$\frac{1}{8}$	$\frac{1}{4}$	$\frac{3}{8}$	$\frac{1}{2}$	$\frac{5}{8}$

8 The coordinates of three vertices of a square are (−1, 4), (3, 4) and (3, 0). What are the coordinates of the fourth vertex of the square?

A	B	C	D	E
(3, −4)	(−1, 0)	(−3, 4)	(−1, −1)	(0, 3)

9 In his pocket, Fred has £1.20 made up of an equal number of five-pence and one-pence coins. How many five-pence coins does Fred have in his pocket?

A	B	C	D	E
1	24	20	30	15

10 20 people eat 50 muffins at a party. What is the mean number of muffins eaten per person at the party?

A	B	C	D	E
$\frac{2}{5}$	$\frac{1}{2}$	5	$\frac{1}{5}$	$2\frac{1}{2}$

11 A regular hexagon has a perimeter of 36.6 cm. What is the total length of four sides of the hexagon?

A	B	C	D	E
36.6 cm	6.6 cm	18.3 cm	30.6 cm	24.4 cm

12 Which of the following is most likely to be the measurement of a woman's height?

A	B	C	D	E
3 km	3.2 m	154 cm	200 mm	1.6 cm

13 This circle has been split into equal parts.

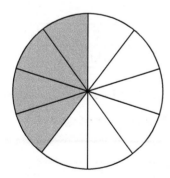

What fraction of the circle is not shaded?

A	B	C	D	E
$\frac{1}{10}$	$\frac{1}{2}$	$\frac{4}{10}$	$\frac{3}{4}$	$\frac{3}{5}$

14 Lucy, Jane, Rahul and Tim run a race. Lucy finishes the race in 54 seconds. Jane finishes 7 seconds faster than Lucy and Rahul finishes 5 seconds slower than Jane. Tim finishes 8 seconds faster than Rahul.

What is Tim's finishing time?

A	B	C	D	E
53 seconds	63 seconds	56 seconds	44 seconds	48 seconds

15 How many oranges that cost 45 pence can be bought for £2.50?

A	B	C	D	E
2	3	4	5	6

16 George cuts a 4.5 kg block of marble into 9 pieces. What is the average weight of each of the 9 pieces?

A	B	C	D	E
300 g	0.5 kg	900 g	450 g	2 kg

17 What is the measurement of the largest angle in this triangle?

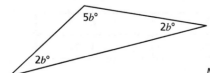

Not drawn to scale

A	B	C	D	E
40°	90°	50°	70°	100°

18 Tara swims 750 m per day from 27th September to 3rd October, inclusively. What is the total distance that Tara swims in this period?

A	B	C	D	E
4.5 km	3.75 km	1.5 km	5.25 km	6 km

19 250 people were asked to choose their favourite colour. 40% of them chose red and $\frac{1}{5}$ of them chose blue. $\frac{1}{2}$ of the remainder chose green. How many people in the group chose green?

A	B	C	D	E
75	125	100	60	50

20 This diagram consists of four identical shaded circles inside a square. The area of 1 shaded circle is 3.5 cm². The square has a side length of 7 cm.

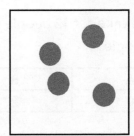

What area of the square is not covered by shaded circles?

Not drawn to scale

A	B	C	D	E
3.5 cm²	63 cm²	49 cm²	35 cm²	14 cm²

21 Amanda bought £6.50 of groceries and paid with a £10 note. What percentage of £10 did she receive in change?

A	B	C	D	E
65%	90%	35%	100%	350%

22 The temperature in London is 14°C and the temperature in Oslo is –6°C.

What is the difference in temperature between London and Oslo?

A	B	C	D	E
14°C	0°C	20°C	6°C	12°C

23 Round 100,045 to the nearest 20.

A	B	C	D	E
100,060	100,025	100,050	100,040	100,020

24 Hannah eats 4 grapes per day and Reena eats 7 grapes per day. How many grapes do they eat in total in a fortnight?

A	B	C	D	E
11	77	56	80	154

25 Point A has the coordinates (4, 4). Point B is a reflection of Point A in the *y*-axis. What are the coordinates of Point B?

A	B	C	D	E
(4, 0)	(4, 4)	(4, –4)	(–4, 4)	(0, 4)

26 Baking a cake for 12 people requires 8 eggs. How many eggs are required to bake a cake for three people?

A	B	C	D	E
0	2	3	8	12

27 60 peaches are divided into three piles with a ratio of $8:1:6$. How many peaches are there in the largest pile?

A	B	C	D	E
32	30	24	4	15

28 There are 40 rats in a sewer. $\frac{1}{5}$ of the rats have brown fur and the rest have black fur. $\frac{1}{4}$ of the rats have long tails and the rest have short tails. What is the largest number of rats that could have black fur and long tails?

A	B	C	D	E
5	10	15	32	40

29 Rectangle A has a width of 5 cm and an area of 40 cm². The width and length of Rectangle B are double that of Rectangle A. What is the area of Rectangle B?

A	B	C	D	E
10 cm²	80 cm²	200 cm²	400 cm²	160 cm²

30 120 students were asked to choose their favourite soup. 20% of them chose chicken and 35% chose tomato. How many students chose neither chicken nor tomato?

A	B	C	D	E
24	60	80	54	60

END OF TEST

YOU HAVE 25 QUESTIONS TO COMPLETE WITHIN THE TIME GIVEN.

Multiple Choice

The questions within this section are multiple choice. Write the answer to each question on the answer sheet by selecting A, B, C, D, E, F, G, H, I, J, K, L, M, N or O.

A $\frac{1}{2}$	B £3	C £3.50	D $\frac{3}{4}$	E $\frac{1}{3}$
F £1.50	G £5	H $\frac{2}{5}$	I £4	J $\frac{5}{6}$

Select an answer to each question from the 10 different possible answers in the table above.

Example i

Tom buys a chocolate bar for £1.50. He pays with a £5 note.

How much change does he receive?

The correct answer is **C**. This has already been marked in Example i for Practice Test 5 on your answer sheet on page 159.

Example ii

Sarah eats $\frac{1}{4}$ of a pizza.

What fraction of the pizza remains?

The correct answer is **D**. Mark this in Example ii for Practice Test 5 on your answer sheet on page 159.

A 24 kph	B 2 hours	C £3.75	D 62	E $\frac{1}{3}$
F 74	G $\frac{1}{4}$	H 9 hours	I 27 kph	J £1.30

Several questions follow for you to answer. Select an answer to each question from the 10 different possible answers in the table above. You may use an answer for more than one question.

1 James goes to sleep at 10 p.m. and wakes up the following morning at 7 a.m.

For how long does James sleep?

2 For breakfast, James eats 4 of the 12 eggs in his fridge.

What fraction of the total number of eggs in the fridge does James eat?

3 James drives to work. The drive takes 30 minutes and covers a distance of 12 km.

What is James' speed in kilometres per hour during this drive?

4 In James' company, there are a total of 97 men and 23 women.

How many more men are there in James' company than women?

5 Before lunch, James has 12 meetings. Each meeting takes 10 minutes.

How long does James spend in meetings before lunch?

6 A sandwich costs £2.50 and a drink costs £1.20.

James buys a sandwich and a drink for lunch and pays with a £5 note.

How much change does James receive?

7 James feels sleepy in the afternoon so he takes a nap for 20 minutes.

For what fraction of an hour does James take a nap?

8 James earns £7.50 per hour.

How much does James earn in half an hour?

9 After work, James drives to the gym. The drive takes 20 minutes and covers a distance of 9 km.

What is James' speed in kilometres per hour during this drive?

10 James brushes his teeth before going to bed every night.

He also brushes his teeth every morning.

How many times does James brush his teeth in August?

A £500	B $\frac{5}{12}$	C $\frac{1}{12}$	D 3 hours	E 200
F 525	G £115	H 42 m	I £12.50	J 14 m
K 400	L $1\frac{1}{2}$ hours	M $\frac{1}{4}$	N 80 m	O 8 hours

Several questions follow for you to answer. Select an answer to each question from the 15 different possible answers in the table above. You may use an answer for more than one question.

11 500 students attend First Primary School. 40% of the students at the school are girls.

How many girls attend First Primary School?

12 $\frac{1}{5}$ of the students at First Primary School have brown hair.

How many of the students at First Primary School do **not** have brown hair?

13 Each student arrives at school at 8.30 a.m. and leaves at 4.30 p.m.

How long does each student spend at school?

14 Maria attends First Primary School 5 days per week.

Each day, she spends £2.50 on bus fares to travel to and from school.

How much does Maria spend per week on bus fares to travel to and from school?

15 $\frac{1}{2}$ of the students at First Primary School are 9, 10 or 11 years old.

$\frac{1}{4}$ of the students at First Primary School are 8 years old.

If I pick one student from First Primary School at random, what is the probability that they are not 8, 9, 10 or 11 years old?

16 Each student at First Primary School has 4 gym classes per week. Each class lasts 45 minutes.

How long does each student spend in gym class per week?

17 The sports field at First Primary School is rectangular in shape. It has a perimeter of 68 m and a length of 20 m.

What is the width of the sports field?

18 Each student at First Primary School spends £1 per day on lunch.

How much is spent on lunch per day by students at First Primary School?

19 Each student at First Primary School spends 2 hours per day doing homework.

What fraction of a whole day does each student at First Primary School spend doing homework?

20 The main school building is three times as long as the annexe building. The annexe building is twice as long as the school's kitchen.

If the kitchen is 7 m long, how long is the main school building?

21 The students in Class A at First Primary School bake cookies and sell them at the school fair. They sell large cookies for £2 and small cookies for £1. They sell 42 large cookies and 31 small cookies.

How much money do they make selling cookies?

22 Henry lives 1.567 km away from First Primary School.

Anish lives 1.487 km away from First Primary School.

How much further away from First Primary School does Henry live than Anish?

23 The lunch break at First Primary School begins at 12:10 and ends at 13:40.

How long is the lunch break?

24 $\frac{1}{4}$ of the students at First Primary School travel to school by bus.

$\frac{1}{3}$ of the students at First Primary School travel to school by car.

The rest of the students at First Primary School walk to school.

What fraction of the students at First Primary School walk to school?

25 Next year, the number of students at First Primary School will increase by 5%.

How many students will attend First Primary School next year?

END OF TEST

YOU HAVE 25 QUESTIONS TO COMPLETE WITHIN THE TIME GIVEN.

Multiple Choice

The questions within this section are multiple choice. Write the answer to each question on the answer sheet by selecting A, B, C, D, E, F, G, H, I, J, K, L, M, N or O.

A $\frac{1}{2}$	B £3	C £3.50	D $\frac{3}{4}$	E $\frac{1}{3}$
F £1.50	G £5	H $\frac{2}{5}$	I £4	J $\frac{5}{6}$

Select an answer to each question from the 10 different possible answers in the table above.

Example i

Tom buys a chocolate bar for £1.50. He pays with a £5 note.

How much change does he receive?

The correct answer is **C**. This has already been marked in Example i for Practice Test 6 on your answer sheet on page 160.

Example ii

Sarah eats $\frac{1}{4}$ of a pizza.

What fraction of the pizza remains?

The correct answer is **D**. Mark this in Example ii for Practice Test 6 on your answer sheet on page 160.

A $\frac{1}{26}$	B 22:37	C $\frac{1}{10}$	D £660	E 25%
F 18:45	G 1.75 litres	H £37.50	I 3.46 litres	J 50%

Several questions follow for you to answer. Select an answer to each question from the 10 different possible answers in the table above. You may use an answer for more than one question.

The Smith family consists of two adults and two children. The two adults are called John and Sarah. The two children are called Amy and James. They live in London.

1 Last year, the Smiths went on holiday to Spain. The cost of an adult return flight ticket was £220 and the cost of a child return flight ticket was half as much as an adult one.

How much did the Smith family spend on flights?

2 The flight lasted for 3 hours. Amy spent 90 minutes of the flight watching films.

For what percentage of the flight did Amy watch films?

3 The time at their holiday destination was 2 hours ahead of the time in London.

If the plane took off at 13:45 London time, what was the time at their holiday destination when it landed?

4 Whilst on holiday, James drank 250 ml of orange juice every morning.

How much orange juice did James drink in 1 week?

5 John bought a new pair of sandals that were on sale for £30. This represented a 20% discount from their original price.

What was the original price of the sandals?

6 Sarah brought £450 in cash to spend on the holiday. After the first day, £405 remained.

What fraction of the cash did Sarah spend on the first day?

7 On the second day, Amy woke up at 07:17 and went to bed 15 hours and 20 minutes later.

At what time did Amy go to bed on the second day?

8 9 out of every 16 guests at their hotel were from France and 3 out of every 16 guests were from Germany.

What percentage of guests at their hotel were from neither France nor Germany?

9 1% of the water in the hotel pool evaporated every hour.

If there were 346 litres of water in the pool, how many litres would evaporate after 1 hour?

10 The Smith family's holiday lasted 2 weeks.

For what fraction of a year were they on holiday?

A 110 kg	B £1,625	C 104 kg	D 80 kph	E 60%
F 60 kph	G 1,728	H £1,500	I 1,820	J £1,584
K 24 kph	L 125%	M 1,200	N 103 kg	O 55%

Several questions follow for you to answer. Select an answer to each question from the 15 different possible answers in the table above. You may use an answer for more than one question.

11 7,000 students began an online course but only 2,800 of them completed it.

What percentage of the students did not complete the online course?

12 Each male sheep produces 12 kg of wool per year.

Each female sheep produces 10 kg of wool per year.

If there are 30 male sheep and 25 female sheep on a farm, how many more kilograms of wool do the male sheep produce than the females per year?

13 The cost of installing a new window is £150. Company A needs to have 15 windows installed. They agree a deal to pay the full installation price for the first 5 windows and $\frac{1}{2}$ the installation price for the rest.

What is the total amount Company A must pay?

14 A train departs from Station A at 16:40 and arrives at Station B at 18:10. The distance from Station A to Station B is 90 km.

What is the train's average speed in kilometres per hour on this journey?

15 Every day, a factory produces twice as many garments as the day before.

If the factory produced 75 garments on Day 1, how many garments did it produce on Day 5?

16 A box contains 2 green balls, 4 red balls, 3 yellow balls and the remainder are black balls.

If there are 20 balls in the box in total, what percentage of them are black?

17 Lucas weighs 120 kg. Simon and Edward both weigh 100 kg. Ian weighs 92 kg.

What is their average weight?

18 The ratio of black mice to white mice in a habitat is 5:7.

If there are 1,300 black mice in the habitat, how many white mice are there?

19 The cost of an airline ticket is reduced by $\frac{1}{5}$.

If the reduced price is £1,300, what was the original price?

20 Bus A travels a distance of 45 km in 30 minutes. Bus B travels a distance of 70 km in 60 minutes.

What is the average speed of Bus A and Bus B in kilometres per hour?

21 The Smith family's gas bill was 10% less than last year's.

If the gas bill last year was £1,760, what was the Smith family's gas bill this year?

22 Sam runs 400 m in 60 seconds.

What is Sam's speed in kilometres per hour?

23 The number of flowers in a garden increased by 20% from Year 1 to Year 2. The number of flowers in the garden increased by 20% from Year 2 to Year 3.

If there were 1,200 flowers in the garden in Year 1, how many were there in Year 3?

24 What percentage is 15 of 12?

25 Round 103,500 g to the nearest kg.

END OF TEST

YOU HAVE 30 QUESTIONS TO COMPLETE WITHIN THE TIME GIVEN.

Multiple Choice

The questions within this section are multiple choice. Write the answer to each question on the answer sheet by selecting A, B, C, D or E.

School Dinners

Some children were asked to vote for their favourite school dinner. This bar chart shows the results:

A	B	C	D	E
pasta	pizza	fish and chips	jacket potato	roast dinner

Examples i and ii

The most number of children said | **Example i** | was their favourite and the fewest number of

children voted for | **Example ii** |.

The correct answer for **Example i** is **C**.

This has already been marked in Example i for Practice Test 7 on your answer sheet on page 160.

The correct answer for **Example ii** is **A**.

Mark this in Example ii for Practice Test 7 on your answer sheet on page 160.

Complete the following questions. Mark your answers on the answer sheet on a separate line for each question number.

Pets

Some children were asked what their favourite type of pet would be. The results are shown in this bar chart:

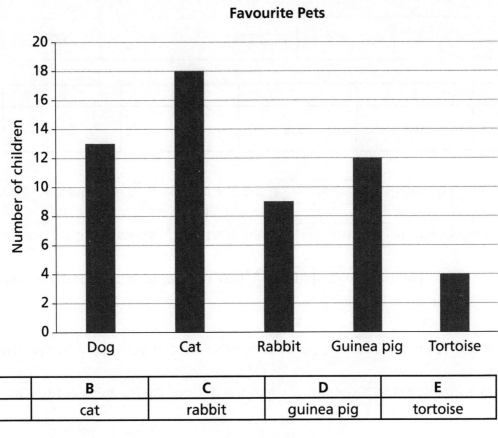

Favourite Pets

A	B	C	D	E
dog	cat	rabbit	guinea pig	tortoise

Question **1** was the most popular pet and Question **2** was the least popular pet.

Three times as many children said Question **3** than said Question **4**.

Half as many children said Question **5** than said Question **6**.

In total, 31 children said either dog or Question **7** and 25 children said either guinea pig or

Question **8**.

Three more children said guinea pig than said Question **9** and eight more children said

Question **10** than said tortoise.

Fractions, Decimals and Percentages

Here is a table showing equivalent fractions, decimals and percentages.

Fraction	$\frac{3}{8}$			$\frac{7}{20}$	
Decimal		0.4			
Percentage			25%		60%

A	B	C	D	E
$\frac{3}{8}$	0.4	25%	$\frac{7}{20}$	60%

The decimal 0.375 is equivalent to Question 11 and the decimal 0.25 is equivalent to Question 12.

The fraction $\frac{2}{5}$ is equivalent to Question 13 and the fraction $\frac{14}{40}$ is equivalent to Question 14.

A percentage of 40% is equivalent to Question 15 and a percentage of 37.5% is equivalent to Question 16.

The fraction $\frac{3}{5}$ is equivalent to Question 17 and the fraction $\frac{5}{20}$ is equivalent to Question 18.

The decimal 0.35 is equivalent to Question 19 and the decimal 0.6 is equivalent to Question 20.

Properties of Shapes

Here is a table showing some shapes and some properties they might have. The table has only been partially completed.

	At least 2 equal sides	At least 1 set of parallel sides	At least 1 line of symmetry
Equilateral triangle	✓	✗	✓
Scalene triangle			
Rhombus			
Parallelogram			
Isosceles trapezium			

A	B	C	D	E
equilateral triangle	scalene triangle	rhombus	parallelogram	isosceles trapezium

A Question 21 has no lines of symmetry and no parallel sides and a Question 22 has no lines of symmetry and at least one set of parallel sides.

Both a Question 23 and an Question 24 have at least one line of symmetry and equal sides.

A Question 25 has four sides and two lines of symmetry and an Question 26 has four sides and one line of symmetry.

Both a Question 27 and a Question 28 have two sets of parallel sides and the sum of their interior angles is 360°.

Neither a Question 29 nor a Question 30 have a line of symmetry.

END OF TEST

YOU HAVE 30 QUESTIONS TO COMPLETE WITHIN THE TIME GIVEN.

Multiple Choice

The questions within this section are multiple choice. Write the answer to each question on the answer sheet by selecting A, B, C, D or E.

School Dinners

Some children were asked to vote for their favourite school dinner. This bar chart shows the results:

Favourite School Dinners

A	B	C	D	E
pasta	pizza	fish and chips	jacket potato	roast dinner

Examples i and ii

The most number of children said ⬚ **Example i** ⬚ was their favourite and the fewest number of children voted for ⬚ **Example ii** ⬚.

The correct answer for **Example i** is **C**. This has already been marked in Example i for Practice Test 8 on your answer sheet on page 160.

The correct answer for **Example ii** is **A**. Mark this in Example ii for Practice Test 8 on your answer sheet on page 160.

Practice

Complete the following questions. Mark your answers on the answer sheet on a separate line for each question number.

Translations

Here are five shapes that have been translated on a grid.

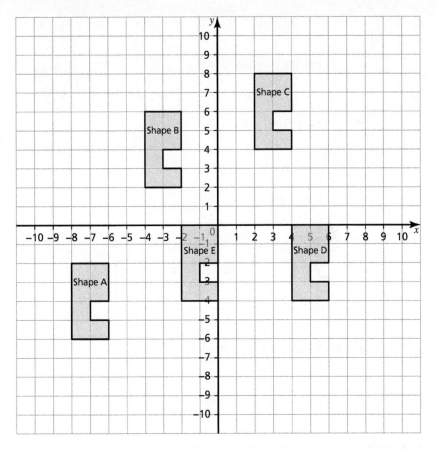

A	B	C	D	E
Shape A	Shape B	Shape C	Shape D	Shape E

Question ① is a translation of Shape A by 4 right and 8 up and Question ② is a translation of Shape A by 10 up and 10 right.

Question ③ is a translation of Shape B by 8 right and 6 down and Question ④ is a translation of Shape B by 2 right and 6 down.

Question ⑤ is a translation of Shape C by 4 left and 8 down and Question ⑥ is a translation of Shape C by 6 left and 2 down.

Question ⑦ is a translation of Shape D by 12 left and 2 down and Question ⑧ is a translation of Shape D by 2 left and 8 up.

Question ⑨ is a translation of Shape E by 6 left and 2 down and Question ⑩ is a translation of Shape E by 6 right.

Factors

This Venn diagram shows composite numbers, factors of 36, factors of 126 and prime numbers.

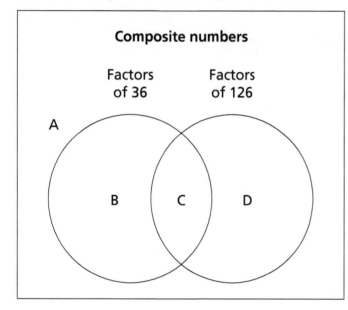

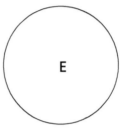

A	B	C	D	E
Section A	Section B	Section C	Section D	Section E

The number 3 belongs in Question **11** and the number 4 belongs in Question **12**.

The number 17 belongs in Question **13** and the number 18 belongs in Question **14**.

The number 8 belongs in Question **15** and the number 9 belongs in Question **16**.

The number 13 belongs in Question **17** and the number 14 belongs in Question **18**.

The number 6 belongs in Question **19** and the number 7 belongs in Question **20**.

Activities

This partially complete table shows the responses of children in four different year groups who were asked their favourite after-school club.

	Gymnastics	Football	Ballet	Craft	Spanish	Total
Year 3	12	15	17		13	85
Year 4	15		24	17	15	83
Year 5	16	17		12		78
Year 6		16		15	17	88
Total	60		78		64	

A	B	C	D	E
gymnastics	football	ballet	craft	Spanish

In Year 3, the most popular activity is Question ㉑ and the least popular activity is Question ㉒.

In Year 4, twice the number of children said Question ㉓ than said Question ㉔.

Overall, the same number of children said Question ㉕ as said gymnastics, and Question ㉖ was the most popular activity overall.

In Year 6, seven fewer children said Question ㉗ than said Question ㉘.

In Year 5, there were 12 children who said Question ㉙ and 19 children who said Question ㉚.

END OF TEST

THIS PAGE HAS DELIBERATELY BEEN LEFT BLANK

Collins

11+
Maths
Assessment

THIS PAGE HAS DELIBERATELY BEEN LEFT BLANK

Collins

Maths
Assessment Paper 1

Instructions:

1. Ensure you have pencils and an eraser with you.

2. Make sure you are able to see a clock or watch.

3. Write your name on the answer sheet.

4. Do not open the question booklet until you are told to do so by an adult.

5. Mark your answers on the answer sheet only.

6. All workings must be completed on a separate piece of paper.

7. You should not use a calculator, dictionary or thesaurus at any point in this paper.

8. Move through the sections as quickly as possible and with care.

9. Follow the instructions at the foot of each page.

10. You should mark your answers with a horizontal strike, as shown on the answer sheet.

11. If you want to change your answer, ensure that you rub out your first answer and that your second answer is clearly more visible.

12. You can go back and review any questions that are within the section you are working on only.

You should await further instructions before moving onto another section.

Symbols and Phrases used in the Tests

 Instructions Time allowed for this section Stop and wait for further instructions Continue working

SECTION 1

 INSTRUCTIONS

 YOU HAVE 20 MINUTES TO COMPLETE THE FOLLOWING SECTION.

YOU HAVE 38 QUESTIONS TO COMPLETE WITHIN THE TIME GIVEN.

The questions within this section are not multiple choice. Write the answer to each question on the answer sheet by selecting the correct digits from the columns provided.

Example i

Calculate 14 + 23

The correct answer is **37**. This has already been marked in Example i in Section 1 of your answer sheet on page 161.

Example ii

Calculate 83 – 75

The correct answer is **8**. Mark this in Example ii in Section 1 of your answer sheet on page 161. Note that a single-digit answer should be marked with a 0 in the left-hand column, so mark 08 on your answer sheet.

STOP AND WAIT FOR FURTHER INSTRUCTIONS

1 Calculate the answer to the following:

$30 - 6 \div 3$

2 Which of these does not exactly divide by 9?

18, 54, 29, 90, 36

3 Which of these is a common factor of 14 and 35?

5, 10, 6, 7, 12

4 In four years' time I will be twice as old as I am now.

How old am I now?

5 How many days in September?

6 How many months are there from 31st March to 31st October?

7 Find the number to replace the '?' which makes these ratios equivalent:

$1 : 9 = 5 : ?$

8 Calculate the number between 50 and 60 which has a remainder of 6 when divided by 8.

9 Which number should replace the '?' in the following sequence?

13, 121, 14, 100, 15, ?

10 Calculate how many tenths there are in the answer to:

$\frac{2}{5} + \frac{3}{10}$

11 If 0.25 were written as a fraction, with the numerator being 1, what would the denominator be?

12 Look at the triangle below:

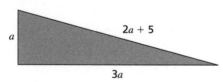

a $2a + 5$ $3a$

If $a = 4$, calculate the perimeter in centimetres.

CONTINUE WORKING

13 If I walk at 3 mph and the bus stop is 0.5 miles away, how many minutes does it take to walk to the bus stop?

14 What is the 15th term in the sequence 114, 108, 102, 96, 90 ...?

15 The fuel tank of my car is currently $\frac{3}{4}$ full. The total capacity of the tank is 80 litres.

How many more litres can I fit in?

16 Calculate the number of 300 ml cups that can be filled from a 1.8 litre bottle.

17 How many quarters of an hour are there in 210 minutes?

18 How many vertices are there on a square-based pyramid?

19 Calculate: $9 + (3 \times 15)$

20 Calculate: $671 - 585$

21 Find the missing number, to replace the '?', that makes this equation correct:

$54 - 18 = 4 \times ?$

22 Calculate the next number in the sequence: 1, 2, 4, 8, 16, ?

23 What is the number if 57 is 6 less than 9 times the number?

24 Which of these is not a factor of 72?

18, 6, 12, 7, 24, 8

25 The ratio of men to women taking part in a charity race is 2 : 3.

If there are 28 men taking part, how many women are running?

26 Look at the Venn diagram showing information about which sports children in a class enjoy.

How many of the children enjoy at least one of these sports?

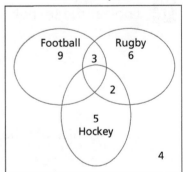

Favourite Sports

CONTINUE WORKING

27 If 0.376 was rounded to 2 decimal places, the answer would contain how many hundredths?

28 Calculate: $-14 + 18$

29 Jackie paid £60 for a guitar after a 25% discount.

What was the original price (in pounds) of the guitar?

30 Find the value of t if: $3t = 28 - t$

31 Andrew has twice as many collector cards as Philip, who has three times as many as Stephen.

If there are 240 cards in total, how many cards does Philip have?

32 Calculate: 87 divided by 3

33 How many eighths of a cake are there in three whole cakes?

34 What is the smallest number of coins from which I could make £2.38 exactly?

35 If nine children received six Easter eggs each, how many eggs is that in total?

36 If the temperature on 5th January was –2°C and the temperature on 12th January was –9°C, by how many degrees Celsius had the temperature dropped between those two dates?

37 There are three times as many staff at Moorlands Primary School as there were 20 years ago.

If there are 24 staff currently, how many were there 20 years ago?

38 I am five years younger than my older brother. In four years' time my brother will be a quarter of my mother's age.

My mother is 44 now, so how old am I now?

STOP AND WAIT FOR FURTHER INSTRUCTIONS

SECTION 2

Example i

Calculate the following:

If I buy five apples at 20p each and four bananas at 35p each, how much change will I receive if I pay with a £5 note?

A	B	C	D	E
£2.60	£3.40	£2.40	£3.60	£1.35

The correct answer is **A**. This has already been marked in Example i in Section 2 of your answer sheet on page 162.

Example ii

Calculate the following:

There are 17 people on a bus when it arrives at a stop. Eleven people get on the bus, and three get off. How many people are then left on the bus?

A	B	C	D	E
28	31	34	25	14

The correct answer is **D**. Mark this in Example ii in Section 2 of your answer sheet on page 162.

STOP AND WAIT FOR FURTHER INSTRUCTIONS

Calculate the following.

1 I add two different square numbers together. Which of these could be my answer?

A	B	C	D	E
8	13	18	23	28

2 I am unaware that my watch stopped at 7.25 a.m., whilst the correct time is 7.35 a.m. Thinking I am early when I check my watch, I stop for a cup of coffee on the way, which takes 10 minutes. My train is due to depart at 7.40 a.m.

How late will the train need to be to give me chance to catch it?

A	B	C	D	E
3 minutes	2 minutes	7 minutes	1 minute	4 minutes

Questions 3, 4 and 5 are linked so that questions 4 and 5 follow on from question 3.

3 A class has 28 children in it. 75% of the children in the class are girls. How many boys are in the class?

A	B	C	D	E
21	7	15	12	10

4 If four new children join the class at the start of the next year, how many girls are there in the larger class if 75% of the children are still girls?

A	B	C	D	E
21	14	24	15	26

5 What is the ratio of boys to girls in the larger class in its simplest form?

A	B	C	D	E
12:18	3:1	4:12	1:3	24:8

Questions 6, 7 and 8 are linked so that questions 7 and 8 follow on from question 6.

6 There are four buses every hour from Lindley to Outlane, with buses departing at regular, equally spaced intervals.

If the buses are always on time, what is the longest I would have to wait at the bus stop?

A	B	C	D	E
Just under 20 minutes	12 minutes	Just under 15 minutes	10 minutes	Just over 5 minutes

CONTINUE WORKING

7 What is the average time I would have to wait for a bus if I arrived at the bus stop in Lindley at random times, during which there were buses every 15 minutes (four buses per hour)?

A	B	C	D	E
12.5 minutes	6 minutes	10 minutes	15 minutes	7.5 minutes

8 If the bus travels a three-mile journey in 15 minutes, what is its average speed for the journey in mph?

A	B	C	D	E
10 mph	45 mph	12 mph	9 mph	5 mph

9 What is the length of time between:

Ten to nine in the morning and half-past three in the afternoon?

A	B	C	D	E
6 hours 40 minutes	5 hours 40 minutes	6 hours 20 minutes	7 hours 40 minutes	8 hours

10 There are 2,374 people in a large secondary school.
1,256 are girls and teachers. 2,194 are girls or boys.

Use the information above to calculate the number of girls, boys and teachers.

A	B	C	D	E
1,076 girls, 1,118 boys, 180 teachers	1,067 girls, 1,181 boys, 114 teachers	1,118 girls, 1,076 boys, 180 teachers	810 girls, 1,067 boys, 164 teachers	1,329 girls, 1,320 boys, 180 teachers

11 Which of these is not divisible by 40?

200, 360, 150, 400, 80

A	B	C	D	E
200	360	150	400	80

12 Calculate the radius of the circle below, which has a diameter of 12 cm.

12 cm

A	B	C	D	E
1.2 cm	31.4 cm	3.14 cm	6 cm	24 cm

CONTINUE WORKING

13 Calculate the mean value of the following data:

8, 3, 7, 8, 3, 6, 5, 6, 2, 5

A	B	C	D	E
4.9	10	3.5	53	5.3

14 Select an expression which describes the remainder of a pie after 3 boys have eaten some. The first boy eats 1 slice, and the second and third boys both eat twice that. The pie is cut into 8 equal slices. The size of the whole pie is P. Each boy eats all the pie they are served.

A	B	C	D	E
$\frac{3}{8}P$	3	P	$0.5P$	$3P$

15 Consider the probability of the following situation:

I roll a dice and it shows a 3. If I then roll a second dice, what is the probability that the total of the two dice will be higher than 5?

A	B	C	D	E
$\frac{1}{6}$	$\frac{1}{3}$	$\frac{2}{3}$	1	$\frac{1}{2}$

16 There are two parallel lines of equal length on a graph. The first line has coordinates starting at (0, 2) and ending at (4, 7). The second line starts at coordinates (3, 0).

Find the coordinates of the end of the second line, if the second point of each line is the same direction from the first point.

A	B	C	D	E
(7, 5)	(6, 7)	(5, 7)	(−7, 5)	(7, −5)

17 If a bag of 60 chocolate raisins is shared between three friends so they have 15 raisins, 20 raisins and 25 raisins, in what ratio have they been shared?

A	B	C	D	E
5 : 10 : 15	2 : 3 : 4	5 : 10	3 : 4 : 5	5 : 4 : 3

18 Calculate and put your answer in its simplest form: $\frac{1}{4} \times \frac{2}{5}$

A	B	C	D	E
$\frac{1}{3}$	$\frac{1}{10}$	$\frac{2}{9}$	$\frac{14}{25}$	$\frac{2}{20}$

19 Calculate and put your answer in its simplest form: $\frac{3}{10} \div \frac{1}{2}$

A	B	C	D	E
$\frac{3}{20}$	$\frac{3}{12}$	$\frac{3}{5}$	$\frac{6}{10}$	$\frac{20}{3}$

STOP AND WAIT FOR FURTHER INSTRUCTIONS

SECTION 3

⚠ INSTRUCTIONS ⚠

 YOU HAVE 16 MINUTES TO COMPLETE THE FOLLOWING SECTION.

YOU HAVE 20 QUESTIONS TO COMPLETE WITHIN THE TIME GIVEN.

A £2.60	B £3.40	C £2.40	D 25	E £1.35
F £3.00	G 14	H 31	I 28	J 34

Select an answer to each question from the 10 different possible answers in the table above.

Example i

Calculate the following:

If I buy five apples at 20p each, and four bananas at 35p each, how much change will I receive if I pay with a £5 note.

The correct answer is **A**. This has already been marked in Example i in Section 3 of your answer sheet on page 162.

Example ii

Calculate the following:

There are 17 people on a bus when it arrives at a stop. Eleven people get on the bus, and three get off. How many people are then left on the bus?

The correct answer is **D**. Mark this in Example ii in Section 3 of your answer sheet on page 162.

STOP AND WAIT FOR FURTHER INSTRUCTIONS

A 10:45	B 60	C 270	D 25	E 10:15
F £1.20	G 128	H 40	I 50	J £5.80

For questions 1–10, select an answer to each question from the 10 different possible answers in the table above. You may use an answer for more than one question.

1 Yusuf leaves home to go to the supermarket at 9:35. He drives 15 km at 30 kilometres per hour and stops to talk to a friend for 10 minutes before entering the shop.

What time was it when he finally entered the shop?

2 Yusuf buys the following to go towards a salad:

spring onions (S) and lettuce (L)

Use the following information to work out the price in pence of one lettuce:

$5S + 3L = 330$ pence

$4S + 3L = 300$ pence

3 Yusuf also sees a special offer on pots of yoghurt. The offer is 'Buy two, get one free'. The normal price is 75p per pot.

How much less in pence does each pot cost with this offer if he gets three pots?

4 There are 8 women working at the supermarket for every 5 men.

If there are 80 men working there, how many women are employed?

5 The supermarket is rectangular and has a length of 50 m. The floor is covered in tiles measuring 50 cm by 50 cm.

If 8,000 tiles are used to cover the floor, how wide is the shop in metres?

6 Yusuf buys some frozen food and needs to get home before it defrosts. The food goes in his trolley at 10:50 but by the time he pays and places the shopping in his car another 20 minutes has passed. His drive home is 15 km and his average speed for the journey is 45 kilometres per hour. It takes 10 more minutes to unpack and put it in his freezer at home.

How long in minutes has the frozen food been out of the shop's freezer?

CONTINUE WORKING

7 Yusuf has arranged to meet some friends for a game of football at 1 p.m. The park is 20 km away and he does not set off until 12:30.

What does his average speed need to be in kilometres per hour if he is to arrive exactly on time?

8 On the way home from the game, Yusuf decides he would like some fruit and calls at a local shop. He buys the following:

Six apples at 50p each and half as many pears which cost 10p less each.

How much change should he receive if he pays with a £10 note?

9 He then notices that half a dozen bananas cost £1.80 but only wants to buy four of these.

How much will he need to pay to buy the bananas?

10 This store has a drinks machine for customers. By noon, the machine had served 120 coffees and 80 teas, and by closing time another 300 drinks had been served, with an equal amount of teas and coffees.

How many coffees were served throughout the day?

CONTINUE WORKING ⇨

A 4	B 14	C 20	D 75	E £750
F £22,000	G £520	H £24,000	I £400	J £20,000

For questions 11–20, select an answer to each question from the 10 different possible answers in the table above. You may use an answer for more than one question.

11 Sarah is having a new kitchen extension in her house. It was supposed to be fitted by 4 men in 7 days. However, only 2 men are available at the time work starts.

If all the men work at the same speed, how many days will it take the 2 men to fit the new kitchen?

12 Sarah borrowed £15,000 from the bank to pay for this kitchen.

If the bank charges interest at 5% each year, how much money does the bank charge each year?

13 The planning for the kitchen began on 1st May and the extension was finally completed on 14th July.

How many days did the project take from start to finish?

14 The floor used to measure 6 m by 3.5 m but is being extended to 7 m by 5 m.

How much bigger is it than before in square metres?

15 The floor is to be covered by large square tiles, each measuring 50 cm by 50 cm.

If the men use 4 boxes of tiles containing 36 tiles in each box, how many spare tiles will there be?

16 The new oven has a discount of 20% as it is in a sale.

If the original price was £650, how much does Sarah pay for the oven?

17 The fridge is also in the sale, and only costs $\frac{3}{4}$ of its usual price.

If the sale price is £300, how much would it usually cost?

18 Sarah plans to sell her house. Before the extension she had the house valued at £200,000. Following the kitchen extension, the value of the house rose to £240,000.

What is the percentage increase in value of the house?

19 The new value of the house is 12 times the price paid when she bought it 30 years ago.

How much did Sarah pay for the house 30 years ago?

20 If it takes 4 years for Sarah to pay back the bank, including the interest, how much extra has she gained financially from this extension?

END OF PAPER

THIS PAGE HAS DELIBERATELY BEEN LEFT BLANK

Collins

Maths
Assessment Paper 2

Instructions:

1. Ensure you have pencils and an eraser with you.

2. Make sure you are able to see a clock or watch.

3. Write your name on the answer sheet.

4. Do not open the question booklet until you are told to do so by an adult.

5. Mark your answers on the answer sheet only.

6. All workings must be completed on a separate piece of paper.

7. You should not use a calculator, dictionary or thesaurus at any point in this paper.

8. Move through the sections as quickly as possible and with care.

9. Follow the instructions at the foot of each page.

10. You should mark your answers with a horizontal strike, as shown on the answer sheet.

11. If you want to change your answer, ensure that you rub out your first answer and that your second answer is clearly more visible.

12. You can go back and review any questions that are within the section you are working on only.

You should await further instructions before moving onto another section.

Symbols and Phrases used in the Tests

 Instructions    Time allowed for this section    Stop and wait for further instructions   Continue working

SECTION 1

INSTRUCTIONS

 YOU HAVE 21 MINUTES TO COMPLETE THE FOLLOWING SECTION.

YOU HAVE 29 QUESTIONS TO COMPLETE WITHIN THE TIME GIVEN.

Example i

Calculate 53 – 42

A	B	C	D	E
12	1	4	5	11

The correct answer is **E**. This has already been marked in Example i in Section 1 of your answer sheet on page 163.

Example ii

Calculate 95 – 75

A	B	C	D	E
21	20	19	18	13

The correct answer is **B**. Mark this in Example ii in Section 1 of your answer sheet on page 163.

STOP AND WAIT FOR FURTHER INSTRUCTIONS

1 What is the number if 48 is four times more than one-third of this number?

A	B	C	D	E
12	20	36	48	96

2 Select the appropriate number to complete the sequence in place of the '?'.

98, 91, ?, 77, 70

A	B	C	D	E
84	86	88	78	83

3 Select the appropriate numbers to complete the subtraction in place of the '?'. Your choice of answers is written as the missing numbers should appear in the calculation from left to right.

```
    5  ?  1  ?
 −  1  3  ?  6
   ─────────────
    ?  4  7  3
```

A	B	C	D	E
4, 8, 8, 9	4, 1, 2, 1	4, 1, 2, 9	4, 7, 4, 9	4, 8, 4, 9

4 The average speed of my taxi journey is 24 mph. The distance of the journey is 2 miles. How long does the journey take?

A	B	C	D	E
4 minutes	5 minutes	12 minutes	16 minutes	48 minutes

5 Hannah buys a dress in the sale following a discount of 20% across all items. It costs her £68. How much does she save compared to the original price?

A	B	C	D	E
£10.20	£17.00	£32.00	£25.00	£80.00

6 Ashraf's father is 38 years old. In four years' time, his father's age will be three times that of Ashraf.

How old is Ashraf now?

A	B	C	D	E
8	10	12	14	16

CONTINUE WORKING

7 Arrange the following in order of size, from shortest to longest.

2,020 mm, 22 cm, 2.2 m, 2.2 cm, 0.2 m

A	B	C	D	E
2.2 cm, 22 cm, 0.2 m, 2,020 mm, 2.2 m	0.2 m, 2.2 cm, 2.2 m, 22 cm, 2,020 mm	2,020 mm, 2.2 cm, 0.2 m, 22 cm, 2.2 m	2.2 cm, 0.2 m, 22 cm, 2,020 mm, 2.2 m	2,020 mm, 2.2 cm, 22 cm, 0.2 m, 2.2 m

8 Calculate $12 \div 0.05$

A	B	C	D	E
0.6	6	24	60	240

9 Calculate 32^2.

A	B	C	D	E
64	128	160	512	1,024

10 Identify the number that the vertical arrow is pointing to on the number line.

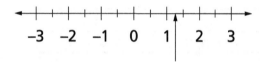

A	B	C	D	E
1.25	2.25	1.05	1.50	0.75

11 Calculate the time that is 2 hours and 40 minutes before 11.25 a.m.

A	B	C	D	E
9.25 a.m.	9.05 a.m.	8.45 a.m.	9.45 a.m.	10.05 a.m.

12 Calculate $\frac{1}{2} \div 4$

A	B	C	D	E
$\frac{1}{8}$	2	$\frac{1}{2}$	8	$\frac{9}{2}$

13 Which number is halfway between 38 and 97?

A	B	C	D	E
66.5	67.5	68	67	135

14 An 'explorer' map has a scale of 1:25,000. The distance between the towns of Dalton and Ulverston in real life is 6 km. How far apart would they be on the map?

A	B	C	D	E
1.5 cm	15 cm	24 cm	2.4 m	1.5 m

CONTINUE WORKING

15 How many grams are there in 2.8 kg?

A	B	C	D	E
0.028	28	280	2,800	28,000

16 Calculate 0.2% of 80.

A	B	C	D	E
0.016	0.16	1.6	40	160

17 Look at the chart below and answer the question that follows.

The chart shows the favourite holiday destinations of children in a class.

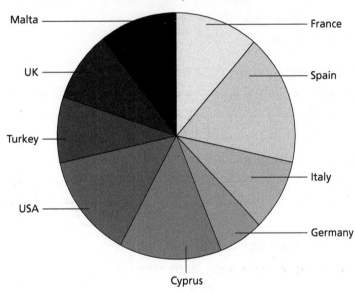

Favourite Holiday Destinations

Which is the least favourite holiday destination of the children in the class?

A	B	C	D	E
Malta	Italy	UK	Spain	Germany

18 A mystery number, p, is doubled and then multiplied by 100. The answer is 400.

Find the value of p.

A	B	C	D	E
0	0.5	80	2	8

CONTINUE WORKING

Look at the chart below before answering questions 19 and 20.

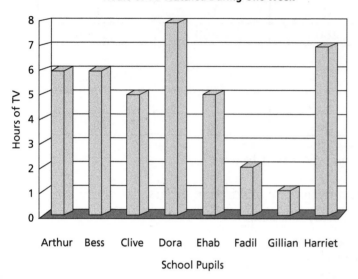

Hours of TV Watched During One Week

19 Which pupil watched the least amount of TV?

A	B	C	D	E
Dora	Fadil	Gillian	Ehab	Harriet

20 What is the mean number of hours a pupil watched TV?

A	B	C	D	E
4	5	6	7	8

Look at the Venn diagram to the right, which shows the number of children owning different pets, then answer questions 21–23.

Pets Owned

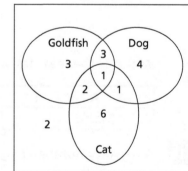

21 How many children owned three different pets?

A	B	C	D	E
0	1	2	4	6

22 How many children do not own a dog?

A	B	C	D	E
9	10	11	12	13

23 How many children own at least two different pets?

A	B	C	D	E
2	3	6	7	20

CONTINUE WORKING ⇨

24 Complete the magic square by choosing the five numbers to go in the place of a, b, c, d and e in the correct order. Each row, column and diagonal adds up to the same value.

a	b	c
d	e	9
6	11	4

A	B	C	D	E
9, 3, 8, 5, 7	9, 8, 3, 5, 7	10, 8, 3, 7, 5	10, 3, 8, 5, 7	10, 3, 8, 3, 7

25 A cinema has 88 people inside. There are 26 adults. There are 70 women and children.

Use this information to calculate the number of men (M), women (W) and children (C).

A	B	C	D	E
M 44, W 18, C 26	M 8, W 18, C 62	M 8, W 8, C 72	M 18, W 8, C 62	M 18, W 44, C 26

26 Look at the quadrilateral, which shows the lengths of each side in cm.

The perimeter = 74 cm. Calculate the value of p.

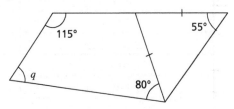

A	B	C	D	E
8	10	28	6	74

27 Look at the quadrilateral and calculate the size of angle q.

A	B	C	D	E
65°	30°	55°	80°	40°

28 Calculate the value that should replace the '?' in this table of currency exchange rates.

GB Pounds	Hong Kong Dollars	Australian Dollars
50	480	90
250	2,400	450
?	8,400	1,575

A	B	C	D	E
2,835	500	3,150	875	300

29 The length of a rectangle is three times the width. The perimeter is 152 cm.

Calculate the length (l) and width (w) of the rectangle.

A	B	C	D	E
l = 60 cm, w = 16 cm	l = 39 cm, w = 13 cm	l = 42 cm, w = 14 cm	l = 57 cm, w = 19 cm	l = 75 cm, w = 25 cm

STOP AND WAIT FOR FURTHER INSTRUCTIONS

SECTION 2

 INSTRUCTIONS

 YOU HAVE 15 MINUTES TO COMPLETE THE FOLLOWING SECTION.

YOU HAVE 30 QUESTIONS TO COMPLETE WITHIN THE TIME GIVEN.

Times Table Test

This table shows some children's scores on two times table tests.

Child	Test 1 Score	Test 2 Score
Amelie	40	45
Babik	48	50
Catherine	43	44
Damon	45	48
Elizabeth	47	48

A	B	C	D	E
Amelie	Babik	Catherine	Damon	Elizabeth

Examples i and ii

| Example i | had the highest score on Test 1 and | Example ii | had the lowest score on Test 2.

The correct answer for **Example i** is **B**. This has already been marked in Example i in Section 2 of your answer sheet on page 163.

The correct answer for **Example ii** is **C**. Mark this in Example ii in Section 2 of your answer sheet on page 163.

STOP AND WAIT FOR FURTHER INSTRUCTIONS

Complete the following questions. Mark your answers on the answer sheet on a separate line for each question number.

Box Office Sales

This graph shows the monthly box office sales of a major film over time.

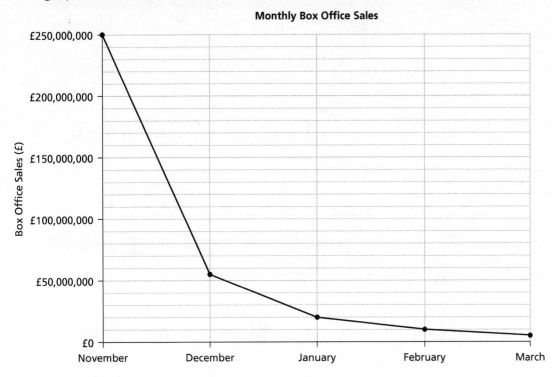

A	B	C	D	E
November	December	January	February	March

The month of | Question **1** | had the highest sales and | Question **2** | had the lowest sales.

The biggest decrease in monthly sales was from | Question **3** | to | Question **4** |.

The smallest decrease in monthly sales was from | Question **5** | to | Question **6** |.

There was a difference of £35,000,000 in sales from | Question **7** | to | Question **8** |.

The total sales of November and | Question **9** | were £305,000,000 and there was a difference

of £45,000,000 between December and | Question **10** |.

CONTINUE WORKING

Converting Units

These graphs show the conversion between litres and pints and between litres and gallons.

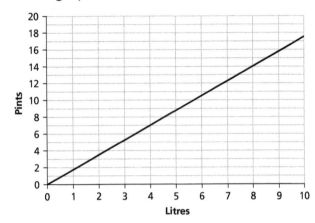
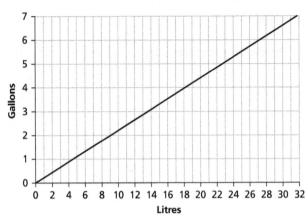

A	B	C	D	E
1	7	3.5	2	10

2 litres is approximately Question **11** pints and 4 litres is approximately Question **12** pints.

1.75 pints is approximately Question **13** litre(s) and 12.25 pints is approximately Question **14** litres.

4.5 litres is approximately Question **15** gallon(s) and Question **16** gallons is approximately 9 litres.

Question **17** litres is approximately 2.25 gallons and 1.5 gallons is approximately Question **18** litres.

6.25 pints is approximately Question **19** litres and 45 litres is approximately Question **20** gallons.

CONTINUE WORKING ⇨

Holidays

720 children were asked where they would most like to go on holiday.

This pie chart shows the results.

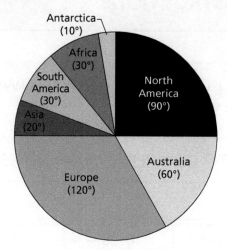

A	B	C	D	E
North America	Australia	Europe	Asia	Africa

The most number of children said they would like to go on holiday in ⬚Question **21**⬚ and the next most popular destination was ⬚Question **22**⬚.

The number of children who chose Antarctica was half the number who selected ⬚Question **23**⬚ and $\frac{1}{6}$ of the number of children who picked Europe said ⬚Question **24**⬚.

The sum of the number of children who chose North or South America is the same as the number of children who chose ⬚Question **25**⬚, and the sum of the number of children who said South America or Australia is the same as the number of children who picked ⬚Question **26**⬚.

120 children selected ⬚Question **27**⬚ and 180 children chose ⬚Question **28**⬚ as the places they would like to go to.

The ratio of children who said ⬚Question **29**⬚ to North America is 2:3 and the ratio of children who said Antarctica to ⬚Question **30**⬚ is 1:3.

STOP AND WAIT FOR FURTHER INSTRUCTIONS

SECTION 3

 YOU HAVE 10 MINUTES TO COMPLETE THE FOLLOWING SECTION.

YOU HAVE 11 QUESTIONS TO COMPLETE WITHIN THE TIME GIVEN.

| A £2.60 | B £3.40 | C £2.40 | D 25 | E £1.35 |
| F £3.00 | G 14 | H 31 | I 28 | J 34 |

Select an answer to each question from the 10 different possible answers in the table above.

Example i

Calculate the following:

If I buy five apples at 20p each, and four bananas at 35p each, how much change will I receive if I pay with a £5 note.

The correct answer is **A**. This has already been marked in Example i in Section 3 of your answer sheet on page 164.

Example ii

Calculate the following:

There are 17 people on a bus when it arrives at a stop. Eleven people get on the bus, and three get off. How many people are then left on the bus?

The correct answer is **D**. Mark this in Example ii in Section 3 of your answer sheet on page 164.

STOP AND WAIT FOR FURTHER INSTRUCTIONS

A 12.50	B 104	C 56	D 3	E 22
F 3,995	G 11.25	H 41	I 26	J 4,950

Read the passage below, then select an answer to each question from the 10 different possible answers in the table above. You may use an answer for more than one question.

Marcus is aged 15 and a pupil at Woolerton School in Kent. There are 5 girls to every 6 boys in his class. There are 12 boys in Marcus's class.

Marcus's sister Ellie attends the same school and Ellie is 11. Marcus notes that if you double his own age, and add Ellie's age, that will give you the age of their mother.

The senior part of the school (everyone aged 14, 15 or 16) all took part in a sponsored run to raise money for a school trip to Disneyland in France. 120 children took part in the run. Marcus's mother sponsored him £2.50 for every kilometre he ran, rounded to the nearest kilometre. Marcus ran for 55 minutes at an average speed of 1.5 m/s.

The school decided to use coaches to take their pupils to France. Each coach can hold a maximum of 45 people. $\frac{5}{6}$ of the senior children travelled to France, along with four teachers.

A one-day ticket to Disneyland costs 50 euros per adult and 45 euros per child. Because of the number of people travelling from Woolerton School, they all received a 15% discount.

40 of the school party rode on the 'Splash Mountain' in Disneyland. Of these people:

- boys and teachers made up 23 people
- girls and teachers made up 20 people.

Marcus boarded the coach to return home at 6.05 p.m. However, some members of the school party were late returning to the coach and therefore they didn't leave Disneyland until 7.01 p.m.

1 How many children are there in Marcus's class?

2 How old is Marcus's mother now?

3 How far, in metres, did Marcus run?

4 How much sponsorship money in pounds did Marcus receive from his mother?

5 How many people in total travelled to France?

6 How many coaches were needed to take everyone on the trip?

CONTINUE WORKING

7 Once in Disneyland, it was decided to split everyone into four groups. Each group had to have one teacher.

How many people were in each group?

8 How much in total, in euros, did the school pay for everyone's Disneyland tickets?

9 Marcus and three of his friends paid a total of 45 euros for their lunch in Disneyland.

What was the mean price (in euros) each of them paid for their lunch?

10 How many teachers rode on the 'Splash Mountain'?

11 For how many minutes was Marcus waiting on the coach before it was able to leave Disneyland?

END OF PAPER

Collins

Maths
Assessment Paper 3

Instructions:

1. Ensure you have pencils and an eraser with you.

2. Make sure you are able to see a clock or watch.

3. Write your name on the answer sheet.

4. Do not open the question booklet until you are told to do so by an adult.

5. Mark your answers on the answer sheet only.

6. All workings must be completed on a separate piece of paper.

7. You should not use a calculator, dictionary or thesaurus at any point in this paper.

8. Move through the sections as quickly as possible and with care.

9. Follow the instructions at the foot of each page.

10. You should mark your answers with a horizontal strike, as shown on the answer sheet.

11. If you want to change your answer, ensure that you rub out your first answer and that your second answer is clearly more visible.

12. You can go back and review any questions that are within the section you are working on only.

You should await further instructions before moving onto another section.

Symbols and Phrases used in the Tests

 Instructions
 Time allowed for this section
 Stop and wait for further instructions
 Continue working

SECTION 1

 INSTRUCTIONS

 YOU HAVE 20 MINUTES TO COMPLETE THE FOLLOWING SECTION.

YOU HAVE 27 QUESTIONS TO COMPLETE WITHIN THE TIME GIVEN.

Example i

Calculate 53 – 42

A	B	C	D	E
12	1	4	5	11

The correct answer is **E**. This has already been marked in Example i in Section 1 of your answer sheet on page 165.

Example ii

Calculate 95 – 75

A	B	C	D	E
21	20	19	18	13

The correct answer is **B**. Mark this in Example ii in Section 1 of your answer sheet on page 165.

STOP AND WAIT FOR FURTHER INSTRUCTIONS ✖

1 Calculate: 32,064 ÷ 8

A	B	C	D	E
48	4,008	408	8,004	804

2 Calculate: $11^2 - 9^2$

A	B	C	D	E
300	40	4	30	20

3 Calculate: $\frac{1}{5}$ of 465

A	B	C	D	E
93	103	91	83	101

4 What is the size of each interior angle of a regular hexagon?

A	B	C	D	E
540°	360°	120°	108°	60°

5 $a = 2b + 3$. Find b when $a = 15$.

A	B	C	D	E
3	6	8	12	15

6 $3x + 2y = 18$. Find x when y is 3.

A	B	C	D	E
4	8	12	6	10

7 $9 + ? \times 6 = 51$. Find the value of the missing number, labelled '?'

A	B	C	D	E
9	5	8	6	7

8 $81 - 7 \times ? = 67$. Find the value of the missing number, labelled '?'

A	B	C	D	E
2	4	3	8	7

9 A box containing 22 packets of sweets costs £3.50. How many packets of sweets can I get with £15.00?

A	B	C	D	E
100	110	66	72	88

CONTINUE WORKING

10 I spin a spinner with five equal sections: blue, green, red, yellow and purple. What is the probability that the spinner will land on red or yellow?

A	B	C	D	E
$\frac{1}{5}$	$\frac{1}{10}$	$\frac{4}{5}$	$\frac{2}{5}$	$\frac{3}{5}$

11 Calculate: $42 \div 6 - 4 + 8$

A	B	C	D	E
4	12	8	11	15

12 Madeleine has 48 guests at her wedding. One-quarter of the guests do not like wedding cake. She cuts the cake into equal sized slices for those who said they wanted it. $\frac{1}{9}$ of the guests who wanted cake leave early and do not get any.

How many guests have some cake?

A	B	C	D	E
32	40	26	35	39

13 What is the missing number in this sequence?   53, 47, 42, 38, 35, ____

A	B	C	D	E
30	32	31	29	33

14 What is two-thirds of 48?

A	B	C	D	E
96	16	32	23	18

15 Ezekial shares a packet of 45 biscuits between 6 friends and himself. How many whole biscuits does each person get if they all receive the same number?

A	B	C	D	E
7	3	8	5	6

16 A grandfather clock chimes every 15 minutes and is silenced for 8 hours at night.

How many times does it chime each day?

A	B	C	D	E
16	32	96	64	80

17 What is the missing number in this sequence?   4, 2, 1, 0.5, 0.25, ____

A	B	C	D	E
0.1025	12.5	0.0125	1.25	0.125

CONTINUE WORKING

18 Twelve people take a driving test on Monday. Four people do not pass it. On Tuesday, 10 people pass their driving test.

How many people passed the test on Monday and Tuesday?

A	B	C	D	E
18	14	10	22	26

19 Which of these is smallest in value?

A	B	C	D	E
38	$\frac{1}{3}$ of 128	one-tenth of 315	half of 65	one-quarter of 132

Questions 20–22 relate to the chart shown below.

Children's Favourite Ice-cream Flavours

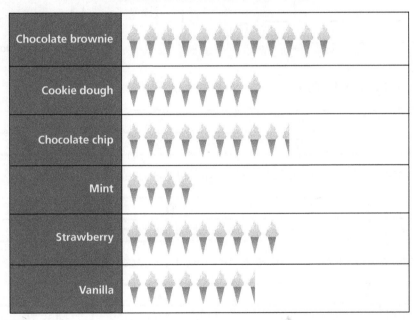

Key: represents 12 children

20 Twice as many children said _____ than said mint.

A	B	C	D	E
chocolate chip	vanilla	strawberry	chocolate brownie	cookie dough

21 How many fewer children said chocolate chip than said chocolate brownie?

A	B	C	D	E
30	60	24	12	18

CONTINUE WORKING

22 What is the difference between the least popular and the most popular flavour?

A	B	C	D	E
108	12	96	24	48

Questions 23–27 relate to the chart shown here:

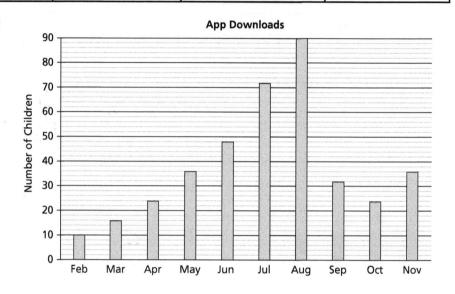

23 How many children downloaded the app in June?

A	B	C	D	E
46	48	42	50	49

24 Between which consecutive months did the downloads change by the greatest number?

A	B	C	D	E
February to March	April to May	July to August	August to September	June to July

25 During which time period did the number of downloads increase by exactly three times?

A	B	C	D	E
April to May	March to June	May to August	February to May	May to July

26 Find the mean number of children per month who downloaded the app over the period shown.

A	B	C	D	E
39	39.8	38.8	38.4	39.6

27 More children downloaded the app in December. The mean changed to 40. How many children downloaded the app in December?

A	B	C	D	E
46	38	41	52	56

STOP AND WAIT FOR FURTHER INSTRUCTIONS

SECTION 2

 INSTRUCTIONS

 YOU HAVE 9 MINUTES TO COMPLETE THE FOLLOWING SECTION.

YOU HAVE 10 QUESTIONS TO COMPLETE WITHIN THE TIME GIVEN.

A £2.60	B £3.40	C £2.40	D 25	E £1.35
F £3.00	G 14	H 31	I 28	J 34

Select an answer to each question from the 10 different possible answers in the table.

Example i

Calculate the following:

If I buy five apples at 20p each, and four bananas at 35p each, how much change will I receive if I pay with a £5 note.

The correct answer is **A**. This has already been marked in Example i in Section 2 of your answer sheet on page 165.

Example ii

Calculate the following:

There are 17 people on a bus when it arrives at a stop. Eleven people get on the bus, and three get off. How many people are then left on the bus?

The correct answer is **D**. Mark this in Example ii in Section 2 of your answer sheet on page 165.

STOP AND WAIT FOR FURTHER INSTRUCTIONS

Several questions follow for you to answer.

A 4	B 127	C £82.00	D 21	E 40
F 34	G £208.00	H 7	I £50.00	J 85

Select an answer to each question from the 10 different possible answers in the table above.

You may use an answer for more than one question.

1 Olivia's class goes on a school trip to the cinema. There are 28 children in the class.

Three-quarters of the class go on the trip.

How many children go on the trip?

2 There must be 1 adult for every 6 schoolchildren who go on the trip.

How many adults need to go on the trip?

3 The school party takes the bus to the cinema. It costs £2 per person (for children and adults).

How much, in total, do they pay for the bus?

4 On the journey to the cinema, there are already 13 people on the bus when the school party boards. At the next stop, 17 more people board and 21 get off.

How many people are on the bus when it departs that stop?

5 Tickets to the cinema cost £10 for adults and £8 for children.

How much, in total, do the tickets cost?

6 The party from Olivia's school is joined by classes from two other schools. One school brings 27 people and the other brings 72 people.

The cinema has 251 seats.

How many empty seats are there?

CONTINUE WORKING

7 The film starts and finishes in the afternoon at the following times:

Start

Finish

How long is the film in minutes?

8 Of the children on the trip, 16 of them buy popcorn and 12 buy drinks.

Popcorn costs £3.25 and drinks cost £2.50.

How much did they spend on popcorn and drinks in total?

9 After the film, the children have an opportunity to stay for a Question and Answer session.

$\frac{2}{3}$ of the children in Olivia's class stay and the rest return to school.

How many children returned to school?

10 The journey to the cinema takes 17 minutes each way.

What percentage of the time was spent on their journey to and from the cinema compared to the time spent watching the film?

STOP AND WAIT FOR FURTHER INSTRUCTIONS ✕

SECTION 3

 INSTRUCTIONS

 YOU HAVE 15 MINUTES TO COMPLETE THE FOLLOWING SECTION.

YOU HAVE 30 QUESTIONS TO COMPLETE WITHIN THE TIME GIVEN.

Times Table Test

This table shows some children's scores on two times table tests.

Child	Test 1 Score	Test 2 Score
Amelie	40	45
Babik	48	50
Catherine	43	44
Damon	45	48
Elizabeth	47	48

A	B	C	D	E
Amelie	Babik	Catherine	Damon	Elizabeth

Examples i and ii

Example ⬛**i** had the highest score on Test 1 and **Example** ⬛**ii** had the lowest score on Test 2.

The correct answer for **Example i** is **B**.

This has already been marked in Example i in Section 3 of your answer sheet on page 166.

The correct answer for **Example ii** is **C**.

Mark this in Example ii in Section 3 of your answer sheet on page 166.

STOP AND WAIT FOR FURTHER INSTRUCTIONS

Complete the following questions. Mark your answers on the answer sheet on a separate line for each question number.

Bus Timetable

Here is a bus timetable for buses between the Train Station and the High Street.

Train Station	13:17	13:47	14:17	14:47		15:17
Library	13:21	13:52		14:54		15:25
School	13:30	14:00	14:30	15:05	15:15	15:34
Playground	13:36	14:08		15:14		15:46
High Street	13:42	14:13	14:43	15:20	15:24	15:54

A	B	C	D	E
Train Station	Library	School	Playground	High Street

The 15:15 bus starts at the Question **1** and finishes at the Question **2** .

The 14:47 bus takes 27 minutes to go from the Train Station to the Question **3** and it takes 26 minutes to go from the Library to the Question **4** .

The shortest time between consecutive stops on the 13:17 bus is from the Question **5** to the Question **6** .

The 13:47 bus takes 13 minutes to get from the Train Station to the Question **7** and takes 21 minutes to go from the Library to the Question **8** .

The longest time between consecutive stops on the 15:17 bus is from the Question **9** to the Question **10** .

CONTINUE WORKING

3D Shapes

The Carroll diagram shows some properties of 3D shapes with straight edges.

	Less than 10 straight edges	10 or more straight edges
Even number of faces	A	B
Odd number of faces	C	D

E – not in the diagram

A	B	C	D	E
Section A	Section B	Section C	Section D	Section E

A tetrahedron (triangular-based pyramid) belongs in Question **11** and a cone belongs in Question **12**.

A cuboid belongs in Question **13** and a square-based pyramid belongs in Question **14**.

A cylinder belongs in Question **15** and a triangular prism belongs in Question **16**.

A pentagonal prism belongs in Question **17** and a hexagonal prism belongs in Question **18**.

A sphere belongs in Question **19** and a cube belongs in Question **20**.

CONTINUE WORKING ⟹

Lollies and Chocolates

Children from five year groups were asked if they prefer lollies or chocolates. This table shows the children's choices.

	Lollies	Chocolates
Year 2	12	15
Year 3	9	10
Year 4	24	16
Year 5	6	24
Year 6	18	8

A	B	C	D	E
Year 2	Year 3	Year 4	Year 5	Year 6

Of the children who prefer lollies, the ratio of Question **21** to Year 4 is 1:2 and the ratio of

Question **22** to Year 6 is 1:2.

Three times as many children prefer lollies in Question **23** than in Question **24** .

The number of children who prefer chocolates in Question **25** is $\frac{2}{3}$ that of Year 2, and the number of

children who prefer chocolates in Question **26** is $\frac{2}{3}$ that of Year 5.

The ratio of children who prefer chocolates in Question **27** to Question **28** to Year 6 is 2:3:1.

The ratio of children who prefer lollies to chocolates in Question **29** is 9:10 and in Question **30**

it is 1:4.

END OF PAPER

THIS PAGE HAS DELIBERATELY BEEN LEFT BLANK

Collins

11+
Maths

Answers

For the CEM test

Answers

Number and Place Value
Page 9: Quick Test
1. 10,065
2. Three hundred and seventy thousand, eight hundred and six
3. a) £224,950
      The 4 in the tens column rounds up to 5 because the digit to the right is 5 or more. All digits to the right of the tens column change to zero.
   b) £225,000
      The 4 in the thousands column rounds up to 5 because the digit to the right is 5 or more. All digits to the right of the thousands column change to zero.
   c) £200,000
      The 2 in the hundred thousands column remains unchanged since the digit to the right is less than 5. All digits to the right of the hundred thousands column change to zero.
4. E
   Newcastle has the highest negative value.
5. 342,950
   342,951
   349,808
   359,806
   359,845   An alternative answer here is '9'.
   The numbers are increasing in value from top to bottom so there is only one possible answer for the missing digits in the first four numbers.

Calculations
Page 14: Quick Test
1. 34
   $180 - (45 + 40 + 61) = 34$
2. 84
   $200 - (67 + 49) = 84$
3. 44
   $308 \div 7 = 44$
4. 3,024
   $252 \times 12 = 3,024$
5. $(76 - 48) \div (12 \div 3) = 7$
   Working out the brackets gives $28 \div 4 = 7$

Page 17: Quick Test
1. E
   12 and 16 are multiples of 4, and 15 is a multiple of 5.
2. Four
   1, 4, 9, 36 are factors of 36 and are also square numbers.
3. 450 seconds
   Find the lowest common multiple of 45 and 50.

4.

10	20	6
8	12	16
18	4	14

Each row and each column adds up to 36.
5. 10
   Carry out the inverse operations:
   $(55 + 8 - 3) \div 6 = 10$

Fractions, Decimals and Percentages
Page 20: Quick Test
1. $\frac{1}{2}$ $\frac{11}{20}$ $\frac{7}{10}$ $\frac{3}{4}$ $\frac{4}{5}$
   Convert to fractions with a common denominator (of 20) in order to compare.
2. $\frac{2}{8}$ and $\frac{3}{4}$
   $\frac{3}{4}$ is equivalent to $\frac{6}{8}$ and $\frac{2}{8} + \frac{6}{8} = 1$
3. $\frac{35}{8}$
   Multiply the 4 wholes by the denominator, then add the numerator:
   $4 \times 8 + 3 = 35$
4. $\frac{6}{9}$ or $\frac{2}{3}$
   The prime numbers in the list are 3, 5, 7, 11, 13, 17. Prime numbers have two factors so 1 itself is not prime.
5. £24
   If Sunita has $\frac{3}{10}$ left after spending £56, then £56 must represent $\frac{7}{10}$ of her money. $56 \div 7 = 8$, so £8 represents $\frac{1}{10}$. $£8 \times 3 = £24$
6. 54
   What is left in the bag is $\frac{1}{3}$ of what was there before Zoltan ate some, so that must have been 6 sweets. That is $\frac{1}{3}$ of the number in the bag before Joanna ate hers, which must have been 18. Finally, that is $\frac{1}{3}$ of what was in the bag to start with, so that must have been 54 sweets.

Page 25: Quick Test
1. A
   Convert each value to a decimal or a percentage to compare them.
2. A
   Convert each value to a decimal or a percentage to compare them.
3. C
   All the others are equivalent to 20%.
4. 75%
   21 out of 28 parts of the grid are shaded. $\frac{21}{28} = \frac{3}{4} = 75\%$

5. $\frac{3}{5}$ (or 0.6 or 60%)
   Three of the five numbers on the spinner are odd.

Ratio and Proportion
Page 28: Quick Test
1. C
   Unlike the others, 24 : 16 does not simplify to a ratio of 4 : 3.
2. 48
   The part of the ratio representing girls, i.e. 3, stands for 18 girls. So each part of the ratio represents $18 \div 3 = 6$ individuals. Since the ratio has 8 parts in total (5 + 3), the total number of children in the choir is $6 \times 8 = 48$.
3. 14.4 m
   If the model plane is 20 cm long, the real one is $20 \times 72 = 1,440$ cm long. 1,440 cm = 14.4 m.
4. 480
   1% of 500 = 5, so 4% of 500 = 20. $500 - 20 = 480$
5. D
   30% of £75 is £22.50, whereas all the others are £25.
6. £1.44
   10% of £1.20 is 12p, so 20% of £1.20 is 24p.
   $£1.20 + £0.24 = £1.44$

Algebra
Page 32: Quick Test
1. A
   If Joyti's brother was y years old two years ago, he is now $y + 2$ years old. In another five years, he will therefore be $y + 7$ years old.
2. 1.5
   Subtract 4 from both sides: $6x = 2x + 6$
   Subtract $2x$ from both sides: $4x = 6$
   Divide both sides by 4: $x = 1.5$
3. 257
   The sequence increases in steps of 4, 8, 16, 32, 64, etc. (i.e. doubling each time), so the next number will be $129 + 128 = 257$.
4. 69
   The number of matchsticks needed is 9 (+14) 23 (+20) 43 (+26) 69. Each time, you increase by the same amount as before, plus 6: (14 + 6), (20 + 6), etc. So the answer is 69.

Page 34: Quick Test
1. E
   If Maya has 4 seeds left over from a packet of 20, she has planted 16. So $4m + 4n = 16$. Of the options available, m must equal 1 and n must equal 3.

2. There are 11 different possible totals (there are 16 possible combinations of numbers but five of these add to the same number, as shown in the table below).

	Second spinner			
+	0	2	5	7
1	1	3	6	8
2	2	4	7	9
3	3	5	8	10
4	4	6	9	11

(First spinner labels the rows 1, 2, 3, 4)

Measurement
Page 41: Quick Test
1. B
   4 hours + 12 hours = 16 hours
2. 5.30 p.m.
   The total length is: 25 minutes + 1 hour 40 minutes + 5 minutes = 2 hours 10 minutes
   2 hours 10 minutes after 3.20 p.m. is 5.30 p.m.
3. £24
   12 × 40 minutes = 480 minutes
   480 ÷ 60 = 8 hours
   8 × £3 = £24 in total
4. D
   The scale shows 1.4 kg. Emily will add 0.8 kg, so it will read 2.2 kg afterwards.
5. 4.2 litres
   The baby drinks 600 ml of milk each day, which is 7 × 600 ml = 4,200 ml of milk a week, or 4.2 l.

Page 43: Quick Test
1. a) 1.2 cm³
   Volume of cuboid =
   length × width × height =
   15 × 10 × 8 = 150 × 8 = 1,200 mm³.
   There are 1,000 mm³ in 1 cm³, so the answer is 1.2 cm³.

b) 7 cm²
   There are three different kinds of faces.
   The top and base are each 15 × 10 = 150 mm²; total: 300 mm².
   The left and right faces are each 10 × 8 = 80 mm²; total: 160 mm².
   The front and back are each 15 × 8 = 120 mm²; total: 240 mm².
   Surface area = 300 + 160 + 240 = 700 mm²
   There are 100 mm² in 1 cm², so the answer is 7 cm².

2. A
   A = 10 × 6 = 60 cm²
   B = 15 × 5 = 75 cm²
   C = $\frac{1}{2}$ × 8 × 12 = 48 cm²
   D = 7² = 49 cm²
   E = 10² − $\frac{1}{2}$ × 10 × 5 = 100 − 25 = 75 cm²
   So B and E have the same area.

3. 12
   This is one way to do it:

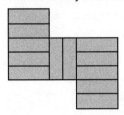

4. 40 mph
   The time taken via the first route is 14 miles ÷ 28 mph = 0.5 hours (30 mins)
   So if the 20-mile journey via the second route also takes 0.5 hours, the average speed is 20 miles ÷ 0.5 = 40 mph.

5. C
   The volume of water in the pond at the minimum depth will be:
   200 cm × 50 cm × 90 cm = 900,000 cm³
   There are 1,000,000 cm³ in 1 m³, so 900,000 cm³ = 0.9 m³ or 900 litres.
   900 ÷ 45 = 20 (this is how many fish can be accommodated in 900 litres of water)
   Zak already has 15 fish so he can buy another 5 fish.

Geometry
Page 50: Quick Test
1. Five
2. D
   Count all the edges shown in the net (19) and subtract the number of edges on a cube (12), so 19 − 12 = 7.
3. 114°
   The known angles in the kite total 42° + 90° = 132°. All the angles in the kite must add up to 360°; that leaves 360° − 132° = 228°. Kites are symmetrical, so x must be the same size as the other unknown angle on the right. So x must be 228° ÷ 2 = 114°
4. (1, 3)
5. C
   (−4, 0) and (2, 3) are exactly two units above (−4, −2) and (2, 1), which are on the line.

Statistics
Page 56: Quick Test
1. 15
   Art = 30 and Drama = 15, so 30 − 15 = 15
2. E
   Read up to the line from 1.5 kg and across to the value in pounds (3.3) on the vertical axis.
3. 165 jars
   15% of the pie chart represents 45 jars of blackcurrant jam sold, so 1% of the pie chart represents 3 jars. Strawberry jam is 55% of the pie chart (100% − 30% − 15%) and 55 × 3 = 165.
4. 6
   If the mean number of merit points scored across 12 weeks was 7, then 12 × 7 = 84 merit points were scored in total across the 12 weeks. Adding up the merit points for the first 11 weeks gives 78, so 6 must have been scored in week 12.

Pages 58–62
Practice Test 1: Numeracy

1. 73
   17 + 56 = 73
2. 60
   120 ÷ 2 = 60
3. 56
   54 − 7 + 9 = 47 + 9 = 56
4. 11
   (12 + 18 + 10 + 4) ÷ 4
   = 44 ÷ 4 = 11
5. 44
   The sequence is +7, +8, +7, +8, +7
   So next term is +8; 36 + 8 = 44
6. 70
   There are 60 minutes in an hour and
   so $\frac{1}{6}$ of an hour = 10 minutes;
   $1\frac{1}{6}$ hours = 60 minutes + 10 minutes =
   70 minutes
7. 4
   15 + X = 31 − 12
   X = 31 − 12 − 15
   X = 4
8. 3
   75 ÷ 8 = 9 remainder 3
9. 60
   1 decade = 10 years; half a decade =
   5 years
   There are 12 months in a year.
   Half a decade = 5 × 12 months =
   60 months
10. 65
    8 × 5 = 40; 8 × 11 = 88; 8 × 3 = 24;
    8 × 7 = 56
    So the answer is 65.
11. 9
    Factors of 36: 1, 36, 2, 18, 3, 12, 4, 9, 6
12. 12
    Calculate in reverse: 8 × 3 = 24
    24 ÷ 2 = 12
13. 15
    74 − 59 = 15
14. 42
    Sequence is +7, +6, +5, +4
    So next term is +3; 39 + 3 = 42
15. 55
    55 ÷ 3 = 18 remainder 1
16. 35
    One whole has four quarters.
    So there are (8 × 4) quarters in 8.
    So total number of quarters = 32 + 3 = 35
17. 16
    $0.5 = \frac{5}{10} = \frac{1}{2}$
    So $\frac{1}{2} = \frac{8}{X}$
    So X = 16
18. 0
    55 ÷ 11 = 5 (no remainder)
19. 48
    1 cm = 10 mm
    So 4.8 cm = 48 mm
20. 1
    $\frac{1}{4}$ of 60 = 15; $\frac{1}{5}$ of 70 = 14
    15 − 14 = 1
21. 6
    (8 + 4 + 7 + 9 + 2) ÷ 5 = 30 ÷ 5 = 6
22. 26
    52 weeks in a year, so 52 ÷ 2 = 26
    weeks in half a year.

23. 15
    It takes Omar 1 hour to run 10 km
    2.5 km is $\frac{1}{4}$ of 10 km
    $\frac{1}{4}$ of 1 hour is 15 minutes
24. 58
    7 + (6 × 9) − 3 = 7 + 54 − 3 = 58
25. 64
    $\frac{1}{4}$ of 256 = 256 ÷ 4 = 64
26. 13
    Sequence is +2, −3, +2, −3
    So next term is +2; 11 + 2 = 13
27. 33
    All sides of an equilateral triangle are
    the same length.
    11 cm × 3 = 33 cm
28. 11
    Last year Bob was 7 so he is now 8
    In 3 years, Bob will be 11 years old
    (8 + 3 = 11).
29. 56
    Kags in 1 Kig = 7 × 8 = 56
30. 6
    Cube has 12 edges and 6 faces
    12 − 6 = 6
31. 88
    579 − 491 = 88
32. 42
    Fortnight = 14 days
    14 × 3 = 42
33. 10
    $\frac{3}{4}$ of a litre = 750 ml
34. 6
    27th Sep to 30th Sep is 4 days
    1st Oct to 2nd Oct is 2 days
    4 + 2 = 6
35. 20
    0.8 kg = 800 g
    800 g ÷ 40 g = 20
36. 0
    $\frac{1}{4}$ of 44 = 11; $\frac{1}{3}$ of 33 = 11
    11 − 11 = 0
37. 99
    123 − 24 = 99
38. 12
    4X − 3 = 45
    4X = 48
    X = 12
39. 13
    Sequence is −8, −8, −8, −8
    So next term is −8; 21 − 8 = 13
40. 66
    Double 36 = 72
    72 − 6 = 66
41. 21
    Area = width × length = 7 cm × 3 cm
    = 21 cm²
42. 61
    Last two months of the year are
    November (30 days) and December
    (31 days).
    30 + 31 = 61
43. 11
    Mean = (Sum) ÷ (Number of terms)
    (5 + 7 + 23 + 12 + 5 + 14) ÷ 6 =
    66 ÷ 6 = 11
44. 10
    −10 + 20 = 10
45. 70
    Cost of rental = £210
    Cost per person = £210 ÷ 3 = £70

46. 15
    45 is five times bigger than 9 so D must
    be five times bigger than 3.
    D = 5 × 3 = 15
47. 8
    Factors of 24: 1, 24, 2, 12, 3, 8, 4, 6
48. 7
    10% of £5 = £0.50 so 40% of £5 = £2
    New price = £5 + £2 = £7
49. 5
    5.9 cm × 7 = 41.3 cm
    46.3 cm − 41.3 cm = 5 cm
50. 5
    50p + 20p + 5p + 2p + 1p = 78p
51. 28
    Total number of sevenths = 4 × 7 = 28
52. 20
    5 × 4 books = 20
53. 5
    Two people in front of him and two
    people behind him so five in the
    queue.
54. 11
    $\frac{1}{2}$ of 88 = 44
    $\frac{1}{4}$ of 44 = 11

Pages 63–67
Practice Test 2: Numeracy

1. 579
   123 + 456 = 579
2. 159
   477 ÷ 3 = 159
3. 103
   32 + 64 + 19 − 12 = 103
4. 58
   Sequence is −3, −5, −3, −5, −3
   So missing term is −5; 63 − 5 = 58
5. 11
   Mean = (14 + 12 + 5 + 6 + 18) ÷ 5 =
   55 ÷ 5 = 11
6. 72
   1 day = 24 hours
   3 days = 3 × 24 hours = 72 hours
7. 10
   11 + 2Y = 44 − 13
   2Y = 44 − 13 −11
   2Y = 20; Y = 10
8. 165
   8.30 a.m. to 11.15 a.m. is 2 hours and 45
   minutes.
   Time spent watching television in
   minutes = (2 × 60) + 45 = 120 + 45 = 165
9. 6
   Factors of 48: 1, 48, 2, 24, 3, 16, 4, 12,
   6, 8 = 10 factors
   Factors of 10: 1, 10, 2, 5 = 4 factors
   10 − 4 = 6
10. 960
    40 × 24 = 960
11. 6
    Area of board = 8 cm × 12 cm = 96 cm²
    Area of 1 square = 4 cm × 4 cm = 16 cm²
    Number of squares that fit on board =
    96 cm² ÷ 16 cm² = 6
12. 48
    $\frac{1}{3}$ of X = 32; X = 3 × 32 = 96
    $\frac{1}{2}$ of X = 96 ÷ 2 = 48
13. 39
    10% of 30 = 3 so 30% of 30 = 9
    Number of birds in tree on Wednesday
    = 30 + 9 = 39

14. 107
$(642 \div 2) \div 3 = 321 \div 3 = 107$

15. 36
Sequence is ascending square numbers so next square number is 36.

16. 2
$\frac{1}{2} + \frac{1}{6} = \frac{3}{6} + \frac{1}{6} = \frac{4}{6} = \frac{2}{3}$

17. 8
$0.4 = \frac{4}{10}$
$\frac{4}{10} = \frac{X}{20}$
$10X = 80$
$X = 8$

18. 3
4.567 rounded to 1 d.p. is 4.6
4.291 rounded to 1 d.p. is 4.3
$4.6 - 4.3 = 0.3$
0.3 = 3 tenths

19. 7
$7X - 7 = 2X + 28$
$7X - 2X = 28 + 7$
$5X = 35$
$X = 7$

20. 36
Work backwards: $49 - 1 = 48$; $48 \div 4 = 12$;
$12 \times 3 = 36$

21. 112
$\frac{1}{5}$ of $80 = 80 \div 5 = 16$
So $\frac{7}{5}$ of $80 = 16 \times 7 = 112$

22. 12
$\frac{1}{2}$ of $96 = 48$; $\frac{1}{4}$ of $48 = 12$

23. 104
52 weeks in 1 year; number of weeks in 2 years = $52 \times 2 = 104$

24. 16
16 cm ÷ 4 cm = 4; 4 plates can fit in 1 row and there are 4 rows in total
$4 \times 4 = 16$

25. 8

26. 26
Tank is $\frac{3}{5}$ full; $1 - \frac{3}{5} = \frac{2}{5}$
So it can hold a further $\frac{2}{5}$ of 65 litres.
$\frac{2}{5}$ of $65 = 26$

27. 27
30th July to 3rd August is 5 days inclusive.
Total growth = 3 cm × 5 = 15 cm
New height = 12 cm + 15 cm = 27 cm

28. 73
Sequence is +2, +4, +8
So difference is doubling each time
So next term is +16; $57 + 16 = 73$

29. 1

30. 976
$6,850 - 5,874 = 976$

31. 26
Fifths in 10 = $5 \times 10 = 50$
Thirds in 8 = $3 \times 8 = 24$
$50 - 24 = 26$

32. 50
$74 - (8 + 16) = 74 - 24 = 50$

33. 20
120 km in 1 hour; $\frac{1}{6}$ of 120 km is 20 km

34. 1,000
1 m = 100 cm = (100 × 10) mm = 1,000 mm

35. 2,938
$3,027 - 89 = 2,938$

36. 150
2.5 km × 2 = 5 km; there are 30 days in November; 30 × 5 km = 150 km

37. 45
$264 - 219 = 45$

38. 1
$3X + 7 = 2(X + 4)$
$3X + 7 = 2X + 8$
$3X - 2X = 8 - 7$
$X = 1$

39. 1
Sequence is –4, –5, –4, –5
So next term is –4; $5 - 4 = 1$

40. 16
Work backwards: $30 \div 3 = 10$; $10 \times 2 = 20$;
$20 - 4 = 16$

41. 1
Days in July and August = $31 + 31 = 62$
Days in October and November = $31 + 30 = 61$
Difference = $62 - 61 = 1$

42. 90
Joey is 15 cm tall so Monty is 45 cm tall and Bruno is 90 cm tall.

43. 343
Total tasks = $7 \times 7 \times 7 = 343$

44. 16
Two years ago I was 11; today I am 13 so in three years I will be 16.

45. 4

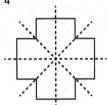

46. 6
100 metres per minute; 60 minutes in an hour so (60 × 100) metres per hour = 6,000 metres per hour.
6,000 metres = 6 km.
So walking speed is 6 kph.

47. 35
Let S be the number of sweets
Remaining sweets = $S - \frac{5}{7}S = \frac{2}{7}S$
$\frac{2}{7}S = 14$ so $\frac{1}{7}S = 7$
Sweets eaten = $\frac{5}{7}S = \frac{1}{7}S \times 5 = 7 \times 5 = 35$

48. 33
Ajit's score = 60%
60% of 50 is 30.
10% of 30 is 3.
So Rom's score = $30 + 3 = 33$

49. 26
$\frac{1}{4}$ of 52 is 13
Number of cards remaining = $52 - 13 = 39$
Cards selected = $\frac{2}{3} \times 39 = 26$

50. 44
7 sevenths in 1 whole
So number of sevenths in 6 = 6 × 7 = 42
So number of sevenths in $6\frac{2}{7}$ = $42 + 2 = 44$

51. 9
9 × £2.50 = £22.50; 10 × £2.50 = £25
So a maximum of 9 caps can be bought with £24.50.

52. 8
1 day = 24 hours; $\frac{1}{3}$ of 24 hours is 8 hours

53. 909
$9,898 - 8,989 = 909$

Pages 68–72
Practice Test 3: Problem Solving
1. E   150 minutes
10 a.m. to 12.30 p.m. is 2 hours and 30 minutes; there are 60 minutes in 1 hour.
So 60 minutes + 60 minutes + 30 minutes = 150 minutes

2. C   144 km
48 kilometres × 3 = 144 km

3. B   145
$45 + 66 + 34 = 145$

4. E   33
One quarter of 44 = 44 ÷ 4 = 11
So $44 - 11 = 33$

5. D   £0.56
Cost of 2 packets of crisps = 22p × 2 = 44p
Change received = £1 – 44p = £1 – £0.44 = £0.56

6. C   9 cm
A regular hexagon has 6 equal sides.
Length of one side = Perimeter ÷ 6 = 54 cm ÷ 6 = 9 cm

7. A   18
Let X equal the number of sweets Tim receives.
Tim : Robert = 3 : 2 = X : 12
12 is 6 times bigger than 2.
So 6 times bigger than 3 is 18, so $X = 18$.

8. B   1

9. E   564
564 is the largest number that rounds to 560, to the nearest 10.

10. D   £32
20% of £40 = £8
Sale price = £40 – £8 = £32

11. B $\frac{7}{10}$
Total number of balls = $7 + 6 + 5 + 2 = 20$
Total number of non-green balls = $20 - 6 = 14$
$\frac{14}{20} = \frac{7}{10}$

12. D   64 cm
Diameter = 2 × radius = 2 × 32 cm = 64 cm

13. E   24
$(22 + 18 + 23 + 33) \div 4 = 96 \div 4 = 24$

14. E   10
The three smallest positive prime numbers are 2, 3 and 5.
$2 + 3 + 5 = 10$

15. B $\frac{1}{2}$
A fair dice has 6 possible outcomes: 1, 2, 3, 4, 5, 6
3 out of 6 of these outcomes are even: 2, 4, 6
So probability of rolling an even number = $\frac{3}{6} = \frac{1}{2}$

16. **A** (6, 6)
The distance between the vertices is 4 units.
Fourth vertex must be 4 units above (6, 2).
So y-coordinate increases by 4.
So fourth vertex is (6, 6).

17. **D** $\frac{5}{6}$
$\frac{1}{2} + \frac{1}{3} = \frac{3}{6} + \frac{2}{6} = \frac{5}{6}$

18. **C** $\frac{1}{6}$
$\frac{2}{3} \times \frac{1}{4} = \frac{2}{12} = \frac{1}{6}$

19. **E** $\frac{1}{6}$
$\frac{1}{2} \div 3 = \frac{1}{2} \times \frac{1}{3} = \frac{1}{6}$

20. **E** $6P$
$D = 3P; F = 2D$
So $F = 2(3P) = 2 \times 3P = 6P$

21. **E** 21 cm
Length = 7 cm so width = 7 cm ÷ 2 = 3.5 cm
Perimeter = 7 cm + 7 cm + 3.5 cm + 3.5 cm = 21 cm

22. **D** 11.47 a.m.
35 minutes before 12.22 p.m. is 11.47 a.m.

23. **D** 6
$4X + 3X = 54 - 2X$
$4X + 3X + 2X = 54$
$9X = 54$
$X = 6$

24. **E** 70 g
£1 worth is equal to 10 ten-pence coins
Total weight = 10 × 7 g = 70 g

25. **D** 54 days
1 litre lasts 3 days.
So 18 litres lasts (18 × 3) days.
18 × 3 = 54 days.

26. **C** 80%
Ken gets $\frac{4}{5}$ of the questions correct.
Percentage = $(\frac{4}{5} \times 100)\% = (\frac{400}{5})\% = 80\%$

27. **E** 45 cm
1.5 m = 150 cm
Length of 1 part = 150 cm ÷ 10 = 15 cm
Length of 3 parts = 15 cm × 3 = 45 cm

28. **D** south-east
180° is half a turn so she will face the opposite of her current direction.
South-east is opposite north-west.

29. **D** −1
One interval on the timeline is equivalent to 1 unit.
B is three intervals after −4.
−4 + 3 = −1

30. **D** 1.5 hours
10 men take 3 hours.
20 is double 10 so 20 men should take half as long.
3 hours ÷ 2 = 1.5 hours

Pages 73–78
Practice Test 4: Problem Solving
1. **B** 9.25 p.m.
1 hour 35 minutes after 7.50 p.m. is 9.25 p.m.

2. **C** octagon
A shape with eight sides is an octagon.

3. **C** 400
$20^2 = 20 \times 20 = 400$

4. **B** $\frac{1}{3}$
She eats $\frac{1}{3}$ so $\frac{2}{3}$ remain.
She gives $\frac{1}{2}$ of remainder to her brother.
$\frac{1}{2} \times \frac{2}{3} = \frac{2}{6} = \frac{1}{3}$

5. **C** £10,000
Ben : Harry : Mia in the ratio 3 : 1 : 2
6 parts in total; Mia receives 2 out of 6 parts so she receives $\frac{1}{3}$
$\frac{1}{3}$ of £30,000 = £10,000

6. **B** 30 cm²
Area of triangle = $\frac{1}{2}$ × base × height
= $\frac{1}{2}$ × 18 cm × 10 cm = 90 cm²
Area shaded black = $\frac{1}{3}$ × 90 cm² = 30 cm²

7. **A** $\frac{1}{8}$
Ginger hair = $\frac{1}{8}$; black hair = $\frac{3}{4}$
Neither black nor ginger hair = $1 - \frac{1}{8} - \frac{3}{4}$
= $1 - \frac{1}{8} - \frac{6}{8}$
= $\frac{1}{8}$

8. **B** (−1, 0)
The square's sides are each 4 units long so you can use this to calculate the missing coordinate. **OR** Each x-coordinate and y-coordinate must combine as the shape is a square so the missing combination is (−1, 0).

9. **C** 20
1 one-pence coin and 1 five-pence coin have a combined value of 6 pence
£1.20 ÷ 6 pence = 20 pence
So there are 20 one-pence coins and 20 five-pence coins.

10. **E** $2\frac{1}{2}$
Mean = $50 \div 20 = 2\frac{1}{2}$

11. **E** 24.4 cm
Length of 1 side = 36.6 cm ÷ 6 = 6.1 cm
Length of 4 sides = 6.1 cm × 4 = 24.4 cm

12. **C** 154 cm
The other options are either too large or too small.

13. **E** $\frac{3}{5}$
6 out of 10 equal parts are not shaded
$\frac{6}{10} = \frac{3}{5}$

14. **D** 44 seconds
Lucy's time is 54 seconds; Jane's time is 47 seconds; Rahul's time is 52 seconds.
So Tim's time is 44 seconds.

15. **D** 5
£2.50 = 250p; 250 ÷ 45 = 5 r25
So 5 oranges is the most that can be bought for £2.50

16. **B** 0.5 kg
4.5 kg ÷ 9 = 0.5 kg

17. **E** 100°
$2b° + 2b° + 5b° = 180°$
$9b° = 180°$
$b° = 20°$
$5b° = 100°$

18. **D** 5.25 km
27th September to 3rd October inclusively is 7 days.
750 m × 7 = 5,250 m = 5.25 km

19. **E** 50
Number that chose red = 40% of 250 = 100
Number that chose blue = $\frac{1}{5}$ of 250 = 50
Remainder = 250 − 100 − 50 = 100
Number that chose green = $\frac{1}{2}$ of remainder
= $\frac{1}{2}$ of 100 = 50

20. **D** 35 cm²
Total area of black circles = 4 × 3.5 cm² = 14 cm²
Total area of square = 7 cm × 7 cm = 49 cm²
Unshaded area of square = 49 cm² − 14 cm² = 35 cm²

21. **C** 35%
Change received = £10 − £6.50 = £3.50
Percentage = $(\frac{£3.50}{£10}) \times 100$ = 0.35 × 100 = 35%

22. **C** 20°C
−6°C to 14°C is 20°C

23. **D** 100,040
Think in terms of multiples of 20:
100,000 100,020 100,040 100,060
100,045 is closest to 100,040

24. **E** 154
Total grapes eaten per day = 4 + 7 = 11
Total grapes eaten in a fortnight = 11 × 14 = 154

25. **D** (−4, 4)
Reflecting (4, 4) in the y-axis means x-coordinate changes from positive to negative and y-coordinate stays the same so (−4, 4).

26. **B** 2
3 people is 4 times less than 12 people.
4 times less than 8 eggs is 2 eggs.

27. **A** 32
8 + 1 + 6 = 15 parts; 60 ÷ 15 = 4
So each part consists of 4 peaches.
So largest pile is 8 × 4 = 32 peaches

28. **B** 10
$\frac{4}{5}$ have black fur; $\frac{4}{5}$ of 40 = 32
$\frac{1}{4}$ have long tails; $\frac{1}{4}$ of 40 = 10
So largest number that can have both is to assume all rats with long tails have black fur, which is a maximum of 10.

29. **E** 160 cm²
Length of Rectangle A = 8 cm
Width of Rectangle B = 10 cm
Length of Rectangle B = 16 cm
Area of Rectangle B = 10 cm × 16 cm = 160 cm²

30. **D** 54
Percentage who chose neither chicken nor tomato = 100% − 35% − 20% = 45%;
45% of 120 = 54

Pages 79–83
Practice Test 5: Problem Solving
1. **H** 9 hours
10 p.m. to 7 a.m. is 9 hours.

2. **E** $\frac{1}{3}$
4 out of 12 eggs = $\frac{4}{12} = \frac{1}{3}$

3. **A** 24 kph
It takes 30 minutes for James to drive 12 km.
60 minutes is double 30 minutes.
Double 12 km is 24 km.
So it would take him 60 minutes to drive 24 km; 60 minutes in 1 hour.
So his speed is 24 kph.

4. **F** 74
   97 − 23 = 74
5. **B** 2 hours
   12 × 10 minutes = 120 minutes =
   2 hours
6. **J** £1.30
   Total spent = £2.50 + £1.20 = £3.70
   Change received = £5 − £3.70 = £1.30
7. **E** $\frac{1}{3}$
   1 hour = 60 minutes;
   $\frac{20 \text{ minutes}}{60 \text{ minutes}} = \frac{20}{60} = \frac{1}{3}$
8. **C** £3.75
   £7.50 ÷ 2 = £3.75
9. **I** 27 kph
   It takes 20 minutes for James to drive 9 km.
   60 minutes is triple 20 minutes.
   Triple 9 km is 27 km.
   So it would take him 60 minutes to
   drive 27 km; 1 hour = 60 minutes.
   So his speed is 27 kph.
10. **D** 62
    James brushes his teeth twice per day.
    There are 31 days in August.
    31 × 2 = 62
11. **E** 200
    40% of 500 = 200
12. **K** 400
    Number of students with brown hair =
    $\frac{1}{5}$ of 500 = 100
    So number of students without brown
    hair = 500 − 100 = 400
13. **O** 8 hours
    8.30 a.m. to 4.30 p.m. is 8 hours.
14. **I** £12.50
    Maria's spend per week =
    £2.50 × 5 days
    = £12.50
15. **M** $\frac{1}{4}$
    Probability that students are 8, 9, 10 or
    11 = $\frac{1}{2} + \frac{1}{4} = \frac{3}{4}$
    Therefore, probability that students
    are **not** 8, 9, 10 or 11 = $1 - \frac{3}{4} = \frac{1}{4}$
16. **D** 3 hours
    Total time spent in gym class = 4 × 45
    minutes = 180 minutes = 3 hours
17. **J** 14 m
    Perimeter = length + length + width +
    width
    Let width = W
    68 m = 20 m + 20 m + W + W
    $2W$ = 68 m − 40 m
    $2W$ = 28 m
    W = 14 m
18. **A** £500
    Total number of students = 500
    500 × £1 = £500
19. **C** $\frac{1}{12}$
    1 day = 24 hours; time spent doing
    homework = 2 hours
    $\frac{2}{24} = \frac{1}{12}$
20. **H** 42 m
    Kitchen is 7 m long.
    Annexe building is twice the kitchen.
    2 × 7 m = 14 m.
    Main building is three times annexe
    building.
    3 × 14 m = 42 m

21. **G** £115
    Total sales = (42 × £2) + (31 × £1)
    = £84 + £31 = £115
22. **N** 80 m
    Difference in distance =
    1.567 km − 1.487 km
    = 1,567 m − 1,487 m = 80 m
23. **L** $1\frac{1}{2}$ hours
    12:10 to 13:40 is $1\frac{1}{2}$ hours
24. **B** $\frac{5}{12}$
    Fraction who walk to school = $1 - \frac{1}{4} - \frac{1}{3}$
    = $1 - \frac{3}{12} - \frac{4}{12} = \frac{5}{12}$
25. **F** 525
    Increase in students next year = 5% of
    500 = 25
    Number of students next year =
    500 + 25 = 525

Pages 84–87
Practice Test 6: Problem Solving
1. **D** £660
   Cost of adult ticket = £220
   Cost of child ticket = £220 ÷ 2 = £110
   Total cost of flights =
   £220 + £220 + £110 + £110 = £660
2. **J** 50%
   3 hours = 3 × 60 mins = 180 mins
   Percentage time spent watching films
   = $(\frac{90}{180})$ × 100 = 0.5 × 100 = 50%
3. **F** 18:45
   Flight time = 3 hours so flight lands at
   16:45 London time
   2 hours ahead of 16:45 is 18:45
4. **G** 1.75 litres
   1 week = 7 days; 250 ml × 7 = 1,750 ml
   = 1.75 litres
5. **H** £37.50
   20% discount so £30 represents 80% of
   original price;
   20% = £30 ÷ 8 × 2 = £7.50
   So original price = 80% + 20% =
   £30 + £7.50 = £37.50
6. **C** $\frac{1}{10}$
   £450 − £405 = £45
   Fraction spent on first day = $\frac{45}{450} = \frac{1}{10}$
7. **B** 22:37
   15 hours and 20 minutes after 07:17 is
   22:37.
8. **E** 25%
   Fraction of German guests = $\frac{9}{16}$
   Fraction of French guests = $\frac{3}{16}$
   $\frac{9}{16} + \frac{3}{16} = \frac{12}{16} = \frac{3}{4}$ = 75%
   So percentage neither French nor
   German = 100% − 75% = 25%
9. **I** 3.46 litres
   1% of 346 litres = 3.46 litres
10. **A** $\frac{1}{26}$
    1 year = 52 weeks; $\frac{2}{52} = \frac{1}{26}$
11. **E** 60%
    $\frac{2,800}{7,000} = \frac{2}{5}$
    $\frac{2}{5}$ completed the course.
    $\frac{3}{5}$ did not complete it.
    $\frac{3}{5}$ = 60%

12. **A** 110 kg
    Total wool produced by male sheep =
    12 kg × 30 = 360 kg
    Total wool produced by female sheep =
    10 kg × 25 = 250 kg
    360 kg − 250 kg = 110 kg
13. **H** £1,500
    Price per window = £150
    5 windows at full price = £150 × 5 =
    £750
    10 windows at half price =
    £150 × 10 × $\frac{1}{2}$ = £750
    Total cost = £750 + £750 = £1,500
14. **F** 60 kph
    16:40 to 18:10 is 90 minutes.
    90 km in 90 minutes is equivalent to
    60 km in 60 minutes.
    60 minutes = 1 hour so average speed
    = 60 kph
15. **M** 1,200
    Day 1 = 75; Day 2 = 150; Day 3 = 300;
    Day 4 = 600; Day 5 = 1,200
16. **O** 55%
    Number of black balls = 20 − 2 − 4 − 3 = 11
    Percentage black = $(\frac{11}{20})$ × 100 = 55%
17. **N** 103 kg
    Total weight = 120 kg + 100 kg +
    100 kg + 92 kg = 412 kg
    Average weight = 412 kg ÷ 4 = 103 kg
18. **I** 1,820
    Let X be the number of white mice
    5 : 7 = 1,300 : X
    So X = (1,300 ÷ 5) × 7 = 1,820
19. **B** £1,625
    Reduced price is $\frac{4}{5}$ of original price.
    $\frac{4}{5}$ = £1,300
    $\frac{1}{5}$ = £1,300 ÷ 4 = £325
    $\frac{5}{5}$ = £325 × 5 = £1,625
20. **D** 80 kph
    Bus A: 45 km in 30 minutes.
    90 km in 60 minutes so speed is 90 kph.
    Bus B: 70 km in 60 minutes so speed is
    70 kph.
    Average speed =
    (90 kph + 70 kph) ÷ 2 = 80 kph
21. **J** £1,584
    10% of £1,760 is £176
    £1,760 − £176 = £1,584
22. **K** 24 kph
    60 seconds = 1 minute so his speed is
    400 metres per minute.
    60 minutes = 1 hour so his speed is
    (60 × 400) metres per hour.
    60 × 400 = 24,000 m; 24,000 m = 24 km
    Speed = 24 kph
23. **G** 1,728
    20% of 1,200 = 240; Number of flowers
    in Year 2 = 1,200 + 240 = 1,440
    20% of 1,440 = 288; Number of flowers
    in Year 3 = 1,440 + 288 = 1,728
24. **L** 125%
    Percentage = $\frac{15}{12}$ × 100 = $\frac{1,500}{12}$ = 125%
25. **C** 104 kg
    103,500 g = 103.5 kg
    103.5 kg rounded to the nearest
    kilogram is 104 kg.

Pages 88–91
Practice Test 7: Cloze
1. B cat
The highest bar is for cat.
2. E tortoise
The lowest bar is for tortoise.
3. D guinea pig
4. E tortoise
4 children said tortoise and 12 children said guinea pig.
5. C rabbit
6. B cat
9 children said rabbit and 18 children said cat.
7. B cat
13 children said dog and 18 said cat.
13 + 18 = 31
8. A dog
13 children said dog and 12 said guinea pig.
12 + 13 = 25
9. C rabbit
12 children said guinea pig and 9 said rabbit.
10. D guinea pig
12 children said guinea pig and 4 said tortoise.
11. A $\frac{3}{8}$
3 ÷ 8 = 0.375
This is a conversion you should know.
12. C 25%
0.25 × 100 = 25%
13. B 0.4
$\frac{2}{5} = \frac{4}{10} = 0.4$
14. D $\frac{7}{20}$
$\frac{14}{40} = \frac{7}{20}$
15. B 0.4
$40\% = \frac{40}{100} = 0.4$
16. A $\frac{3}{8}$
3 ÷ 8 = 0.375 = 37.5%
17. E 60%
$\frac{3}{5} = \frac{60}{100} = 60\%$
18. C 25%
$\frac{5}{20} = \frac{25}{100} = 25\%$
19. D $\frac{7}{20}$
$0.35 = \frac{35}{100} = \frac{7}{20}$
20. E 60%
0.6 × 100 = 60%
21. B scalene triangle
22. D parallelogram
23. C rhombus
24. A equilateral triangle
25. C rhombus
26. E isosceles trapezium
27. D parallelogram
28. C rhombus
(answers to 27 and 28 can be in either order)
29. B scalene triangle
30. D parallelogram
(answers to 29 and 30 can be in either order)

Pages 92–95
Practice Test 8: Cloze
1. B Shape B
Moving Shape A by 4 right and 8 up gets to Shape B.
2. C Shape C
Moving Shape A by 10 up and 10 right gets to Shape C.
3. D Shape D
Moving Shape B by 8 right and 6 down gets to Shape D.
4. E Shape E
Moving Shape B by 2 right and 6 down gets to Shape E.
5. E Shape E
Moving Shape C by 4 left and 8 down gets to Shape E.
6. B Shape B
Moving Shape C by 6 left and 2 down gets to Shape B.
7. A Shape A
Moving Shape D by 12 left and 2 down gets to Shape A.
8. C Shape C
Moving Shape D by 2 left and 8 up gets to Shape C.
9. A Shape A
Moving Shape E by 6 left and 2 down gets to Shape A.
10. D Shape D
Moving Shape E by 6 right gets to Shape D.
11. C Section C
3 is a factor of both 36 and 126.
12. B Section B
4 is a factor of 36, but not 126.
13. E Section E
17 is a prime number.
14. C Section C
18 is a factor of both 36 and 126.
15. A Section A
8 is a composite number that is not a factor of 36 or 126.
16. C Section C
9 is a factor of both 36 and 126.
17. E Section E
13 is a prime number.
18. D Section D
14 is a factor of 126 but not 36.
19. C Section C
6 is a factor of both 36 and 126.
20. E Section E
7 is a prime number.
21. D craft
28 children said craft.
22. A gymnastics
12 children said gymnastics.
23. C ballet
24. B football
12 children said football and 24 said ballet.
25. B football
60 children said gymnastics and 60 said football.
26. C ballet
27. B football
28. C ballet
16 children said football and 23 said ballet.
29. D craft
30. E Spanish

ASSESSMENT PAPER 1
Pages 100–103: Section 1
1. 28
   Using correct order of operations, divide 6 by 3 first, then subtract from 30.
2. 29
   There will be a remainder of 2.
3. 7
   $14 \div 7 = 2$ and $35 \div 7 = 5$.
4. 4
   If n is my age now, $n + 4 = n + n$, so n must equal 4.
5. 30
6. 7
7. 45
   $5 \times 9 = 45$
8. 54
   We are looking for a number that is 6 more than a multiple of 8 and between 50 and 60. The nearest multiple of 8 below 50 is 48, so now add 6.
9. 81
   There are two alternating sequences: whole numbers increasing from 13, and square numbers decreasing from 121.
10. 7
    Convert $\frac{2}{5}$ to $\frac{4}{10}$, then add 3 more tenths.
11. 4
    0.25 is one-quarter.
12. 29
    The perimeter is $6a + 5$, so $6 \times 4 = 24$; add 5 to give 29.
13. 10
    0.5 is one-sixth of 3, and one-sixth of an hour is 10 minutes.
14. 30
    Each term decreases by 6 so the starting term must be 120. Use the formula $120 - 6n$, where $n = 15$ and 6×15 gives 90, then subtract from 120.
15. 20
    Three-quarters of 80 is 60, so there is room for another 20 litres.
16. 6
    1.8 litres = 1,800 ml, so divide this by 300.
17. 14
    Quarter of an hour = 15 minutes, so divide 210 by 15.
18. 5
    Vertices are corners. There are four on the square base, plus the one they all join to at the top.
19. 54
    First calculate the brackets, which gives 45, then add 9.
20. 86
21. 9
    $54 - 18 = 36$, then divide by 4.
22. 32
    These are successive powers of 2; in other words, the numbers double each time.
23. 7
    Add 6 to 57, then divide by 9.
24. 7
    There would be a remainder of 2.
25. 42
    Divide 28 men by 2, then multiply by 3.
26. 25
    All but 4 enjoy at least one sport.

27. 8
    0.376 would become 0.38 to 2 decimal places.
28. 4
29. 80
    £60 is $\frac{3}{4}$ of the original price, so divide by 3 then multiply by 4.
30. 7
    Add t to both sides; $4t = 28$, so divide by 4.
31. 72
    Say Stephen has x cards, then Philip has $3x$ and Andrew has $6x$. This gives $10x = 240$, meaning Stephen has 24 cards and Philip has 3 times more.
32. 29
33. 24
    Eight pieces multiplied by 3.
34. 6
    Coins required: £2, 20p, 10p, 5p, 2p, 1p.
35. 54
36. 7
37. 8
    $24 \div 3 = 8$
38. 3
    In four years, my mother will be 48, so my brother will be 12. As I am five years younger, I will be 7, which means I must be 3 years old now.

Pages 104–107: Section 2
1. B 13
   $4 + 9 = 13$
2. C 7 minutes
   I finish my drink at 7.45, so the train has to leave after that at 7.47
3. B 7
   25% are boys, which is $\frac{1}{4}$ of 28.
4. C 24
   The class now has 32 pupils and $\frac{3}{4}$ of that is 24.
5. D 1:3
   There are three times as many girls, but the question asks for the boys' value first.
6. C Just under 15 minutes
   Four buses in an hour means 1 every 15 minutes, so if you just missed one, you should only be waiting a little less than 15 minutes for the next one.
7. E 7.5 minutes
   The average of 0 to 15 minutes.
8. C 12 mph
   Multiply by 4, so 3 miles in 15 minutes means 12 miles in 60 minutes (1 hour).
9. A 6 hours 40 minutes
   10 minutes to 9 a.m., then 6 hours and an extra 30 minutes.
10. A 1,076 girls, 1,118 boys, 180 teachers
    Boys = 2,374 (total) – 1,256 (girls and teachers) = 1,118
11. C 150
    There would be a remainder of 30.
12. D 6 cm
    Radius is half the diameter.
13. E 5.3
    Divide the total by how many items to find the mean, so $53 \div 10$.
14. A $\frac{3}{8}P$
    The boys eat $1 + 2 + 2 = 5$ slices, so 3 are left out of 8.

15. C $\frac{2}{3}$
    To total more than 5, you need to roll 3, 4, 5 or 6 on the second dice: $\frac{4}{6} = \frac{2}{3}$
16. A (7, 5)
    The line moves along 4 and up 5, so add that to (3, 0).
17. D 3:4:5
    Simplify by dividing by 5.
18. B $\frac{1}{10}$
    Multiplying top by top and bottom by bottom gives $\frac{2}{20}$, which simplifies to $\frac{1}{10}$.
19. C $\frac{3}{5}$
    Dividing by $\frac{1}{2}$ is the same as multiplying by 2, giving $\frac{6}{10}$. Then simplify.

Pages 108–112: Section 3
1. E 10:15
   Half an hour driving takes him to 10:05, plus 10 minutes talking.
2. B 60
   An extra spring onion costs 30p, so four cost 120p, which allows 180p for three lettuces.
3. D 25
   The offer on three pots costs £1.50 in total, so 50p each compared to 75p normally.
4. G 128
   $80 \div 5 = 16$, and $16 \times 8 = 128$.
5. H 40
   It takes 4 tiles to make 1 square metre, so the area of the shop must be 2,000 m².
6. I 50
   The drive home takes 20 minutes, then add 20 and 10.
7. H 40
   He needs to cover 20 km in 30 minutes which scales up to 40 km in an hour.
8. J £5.80
   £3 for apples plus three pears, at 40p each, amounts to £4.20.
9. F £1.20
   Each banana costs 30p.
10. C 270
    An extra 150 coffees after noon, added to the 120 earlier.
11. B 14
    Half the men will take twice as long to fit.
12. E £750
    1% of 15,000 is £150, and $5 \times 150 = 750$.
13. D 75
    May has 31 days, June has 30, plus 14 in July.
14. B 14
    $6 \times 3.5 = 21$, and $7 \times 5 = 35$. Then subtract.
15. A 4
    4 tiles make 1m²; $4 \times 35 = 140$ tiles required.
    $4 \times 36 = 144$, so 4 left over.
16. G £520
    10% of 650 = 65, so 20% = 130. Subtract this from 650.
17. I £400
    $\frac{1}{4}$ must be worth £100, so multiply this by 4.

18. **C** 20
40,000 out of 200,000 is the same as 20,000 out of 100,000 or 20 out of 100 (20%).
19. **J** £20,000
240,000 ÷ 12
20. **F** £22,000
4 years' interest = 4 × 750 = 3,000, plus the £15,000 borrowed means it cost her £18,000. However, the value of the house increased by £40,000, so an overall gain of £22,000.

ASSESSMENT PAPER 2
Pages 114–119: Section 1
1. **C** 36
One-third of 36 is 12, and four times 12 is 48.
2. **A** 84
The sequence decreases by 7 each time, and 91 − 7 = 84.
3. **E** 4, 8, 4, 9
In the ones column, 9 − 6 = 3, so the last number is 9. In the tens column, the answer is 7, so you would have borrowed one to give 11 − 4 = 7. In the hundreds column, 7 − 3 = 4, but you have already borrowed 1, so this question mark must be 8.
4. **B** 5 minutes
Speed = Distance ÷ Time,
so Time = Distance ÷ Speed
$\frac{2}{24} = \frac{1}{12}$ hour
$\frac{1}{12}$ hour is $\frac{60}{12}$ = 5 minutes
5. **B** £17.00
£68 is 80% of the original price, so the original price is £68 ÷ 8 × 10 = £85. Hannah therefore saves £85 − £68 = £17.00
6. **B** 10
In four years' time, Ashraf's father will be 42.
$\frac{1}{3}$ of 42 is 14, so Ashraf will be 14.
Therefore Ashraf is currently 10.
7. **D** 2.2 cm, 0.2 m, 22 cm, 2,020 mm, 2.2 m
There are 10 mm in 1 cm and 100 cm in 1 m.
Change everything to cm, so you get 202, 22, 220, 2.2, 20.
8. **E** 240
Multiply both numbers by 100 to get 1,200 ÷ 5, which is 240.
9. **E** 1,024
30 × 32 = 960 and 2 × 32 = 64
960 + 64 = 1,024
10. **A** 1.25
Midway between 1 and 1.5
11. **C** 8.45 a.m.
Subtract three hours from 11.25 a.m. to give 8.25 a.m.
Then add on 20 minutes to give 8.45 a.m.
12. **A** $\frac{1}{8}$
To make the fraction four times smaller, you multiply the denominator by 4.
13. **B** 67.5
38 + 97 = 135 and 135 ÷ 2 = 67.5

14. **C** 24 cm
6 km = 6,000 m = 600,000 cm
600,000 ÷ 25,000 = 24 cm
15. **D** 2,800
There are 1,000 g in 1 kg. So 2.8 kg = 2.8 × 1,000 = 2,800 g.
16. **B** 0.16
0.2% of 80 is $\frac{0.2}{100}$ × 80
= $\frac{2}{1,000}$ × 80 = $\frac{160}{1,000}$ = 0.16
17. **E** Germany
The smallest sector in the pie chart represents Germany.
18. **D** 2
Doubling p gives you $2p$.
$2p$ × 100 = $200p$
$200p$ = 400, so p = 2.
19. **C** Gillian
The lowest bar in the bar chart represents Gillian.
20. **B** 5
To find the mean, you find the total number of hours and divide by the number of pupils.
So 40 ÷ 8 = 5.
21. **B** 1
The overlap of the three circles represents children owning three pets, so the answer is 1.
22. **E** 13
Adding all the numbers 'outside' the dog circle, you get 6 + 2 + 3 + 2 = 13.
23. **D** 7
'At least two pets' is everything inside the four overlapping parts of the Venn diagram.
2 + 1 + 3 + 1 = 7
24. **D** 10, 3, 8, 5, 7
Adding the numbers in the bottom row gives a total of 21. So the top right-hand number must be 8, as 8 + 9 + 4 = 21. Then the middle number e must be 7, since 6 + 7 + 8 = 21. Therefore b = 3 and hence a = 10.
25. **D** M 18, W 8, C 62
88 − 26 = 62, so there are 62 children. Therefore there are 70 − 62 = 8 women.
Since there are 88 people altogether, there must be 18 men, since 62 + 8 + 18 = 88.
26. **A** 8
The perimeter is the sum of the sides.
$9p$ + 2 = 74, so $9p$ = 72 and p = 8.
27. **C** 55°
Base angles in an isosceles triangle are the same. In this case (the right-hand triangle part), there are two base angles of 55°. So the angle next to the 80° is 55°. The sum of the interior angles of a quadrilateral is 360°, so 115 + 55 + 135 + q = 360.
305 + q = 360. Therefore q = 55.
28. **D** 875
£250 = 2,400 Hong Kong Dollars
So 8,400 Hong Kong Dollars will be more than £500 but less than £1,000.
29. **D** l = 57 cm, w = 19 cm
If the width is w, then the length is $3w$. So the perimeter is $3w$ + $3w$ + w + w = 152.
$8w$ = 152, so w = 19 cm.
Also, l = $3w$ = 3 × 19 cm = 57 cm.

Pages 120–123: Section 2
1. **A** November
The highest point on the graph is November.
2. **E** March
The lowest point on the graph is March.
3. **A** November
4. **B** December
The graph has the steepest decline between November and December.
5. **D** February
6. **E** March
The graph has the least steep decline between February and March.
7. **B** December
8. **C** January
December had £55,000,000 and January had £20,000,000.
9. **B** December
November had £250,000,000 of sales and December had £55,000,000.
10. **D** February
December had £55,000,000 and February had £10,000,000.
11. **C** 3.5
Read up from 2 litres to the line, then read across to 3.5 pints.
12. **B** 7
Read up from 4 litres to the line, then read across to 7 pints.
13. **A** 1
Read across from 1.75 pints, then read down to 1 litre.
14. **B** 7
Read across from 12.25 pints, then read down to 7 litres.
15. **A** 1
Read up from 4.5 litres to the line, then read across to 1 gallon.
16. **D** 2
Read up from 9 litres to the line, then read across to 2 gallons.
17. **E** 10
Read across from 2.25 gallons to the line, then read down to 10 litres.
18. **B** 7
Read across from 1.5 gallons to the line, then read down to 7 litres.
19. **C** 3.5
Read across from 6.25 pints, then read down to 3.5 litres.
20. **E** 10
Look at the litres and gallons conversion graph. 1 gallon is approximately 4.5 litres, so 45 litres is approximately 10 gallons.
21. **C** Europe
Europe is the largest section of the pie chart.
22. **A** North America
North America is the second largest section of the pie chart.
23. **D** Asia
The Asia segment on the pie chart is twice the size of the Antarctica segment.
24. **D** Asia
The Europe segment is six times the size of the Asia segment.
25. **C** Europe
The areas of North and South America combined are the same as the area of Europe on the pie chart.

26. **A** North America
The areas of South America and Australia combined are the same as the area of North America on the pie chart.
27. **B** Australia
720 children were surveyed so each degree on the pie chart represents 2 children. Australia is 60°, so 120 children said Australia.
28. **A** North America
720 children were surveyed so each degree on the pie chart represents 2 children. North America is 90°, so 180 children said North America.
29. **B** Australia
Australia is 60° on the pie chart and North America is 90°, a ratio of 60:90 (or 2:3).
30. **E** Africa
Antarctica is 10° on the pie chart and Africa is 30°, a ratio of 10:30 (or 1:3).

Pages 124–126: Section 3
1. **E** 22
There are 12 boys, so 10 girls.
The total is 12 + 10 = 22
2. **H** 41
15 × 2 + 11 = 41
3. **J** 4,950
55 minutes = 55 × 60 = 3,300 seconds
Distance = Speed × Time
Distance = 1.5 × 3,300 = 4,950 m
4. **A** 12.50
£2.50 × 5 = £12.50
5. **B** 104
$\frac{5}{6}$ × 120 = 100.
100 pupils + 4 teachers = 104
6. **D** 3
2 × 45 = 90 and 3 × 45 = 135, so 3 coaches are needed.
7. **I** 26
104 ÷ 4 = 26
8. **F** 3,995
(50 × 4) + (100 × 45) = 4,700 euros
85% of 4,700 = 3,995 euros
9. **G** 11.25
45 ÷ 4 = 11.25
10. **D** 3
23 + 20 = 43 people, but the number of teachers has been counted twice. Since 40 people rode the 'Splash Mountain', this means there were 3 teachers.
11. **C** 56
There are 56 minutes from 6.05 p.m. to 7.01 p.m.

ASSESSMENT PAPER 3
Pages 128–132: Section 1
1. **B** 4,008
To estimate the answer quickly, work out 32,000 ÷ 8.
2. **B** 40
121 − 81 = 40
3. **A** 93
465 ÷ 5 = 93
4. **C** 120°
The sum of the exterior angles of any polygon is 360°.
Exterior: 360° ÷ 6 = 60°
Interior + Exterior = 180°
Interior: 180° − 60° = 120°

5. **B** 6
Substitute a = 15:   15 = 2b + 3
Rearrange: 2b = 15 − 3
Solve for b: 2b = 12, so b = 6
6. **A** 4
Substitute y = 3:   3x + (2 × 3) = 18
Rearrange: 3x = 18 − 6
Solve for x: 3x = 12, so x = 4
7. **E** 7
9 + 42 = 51, so ? = 7
8. **A** 2
81 − 14 = 67, so ? = 2
9. **E** 88
15 ÷ 3.5 = 4 r1, so I can buy 4 boxes.
4 × 22 = 88
10. **D** $\frac{2}{5}$
There is 1 red and 1 yellow section.
There are 5 sections in total.
The probability of red or yellow is $\frac{2}{5}$.
11. **D** 11
42 ÷ 6 = 7
7 − 4 + 8 = 11
12. **A** 32
48 ÷ 4 = 12 guests did not want cake.
48 − 12 = 36 guests said they wanted cake.
36 ÷ 9 = 4 guests left early.
36 − 4 = 32 guests have cake.
13. **E** 33
The sequence is decreasing by 6, then 5, then 4, then 3. The next term will be decreased by 2.
35 − 2 = 33
14. **C** 32
48 ÷ 3 = 16
16 × 2 = 32
15. **E** 6
45 ÷ 7 = 6 r3, so each person can have 6 biscuits with 3 remaining.
16. **D** 64
60 ÷ 15 = 4 chimes each hour
24 − 8 = 16 hours
16 × 4 = 64 chimes each day
17. **E** 0.125
Each term is divided by 2.
0.25 ÷ 2 = 0.125
18. **A** 18
12 − 4 = 8 people passed on Monday
8 + 10 = 18
19. **C** one-tenth of 315
A = 38
B = 128 ÷ 3 = 42 r2
C = 315 ÷ 10 = 31.5
D = 65 ÷ 2 = 32.5
E = 132 ÷ 4 = 33
20. **E** cookie dough
Mint has 4 ice-cream cones and cookie dough has 8.
21. **A** 30
Each ice-cream cone represents 12 children.
Chocolate brownie has 2.5 more ice-cream cones.
2.5 × 12 = 30
22. **C** 96
Mint has the least and chocolate brownie has the most.
Chocolate brownie has 8 more ice-cream cones than mint.
8 × 12 = 96
23. **B** 48
24. **D** August to September

25. **B** March to June
16 children downloaded the app in March.
48 children downloaded the app in June.
16 × 3 = 48
26. **C** 38.8
The sum of the number of downloads is 388.
388 ÷ 10 = 38.8
27. **D** 52
For the mean to be 40, the sum must be 40 × 11 = 440.
The sum of the first ten months is 388.
440 − 388 = 52

Pages 133–135: Section 2
1. **D** 21
28 ÷ 4 = 7
7 × 3 = 21
2. **A** 4
21 ÷ 6 = 3.5, so there must be 4 adults.
3. **I** £50.00
There are 25 people in total.
25 × £2 = £50.00
4. **F** 34
13 + 25 = 38
38 + 17 − 21 = 34
5. **G** £208.00
£10 × 4 = £40.00
£8 × 21 = £168.00
£40 + £168 = £208.00
6. **B** 127
25 + 27 + 72 = 124
251 − 124 = 127
7. **J** 85
12.50 p.m. to 2.15 p.m. is 1 hour and 25 minutes, or 85 minutes.
8. **C** £82.00
16 × £3.25 = £52.00
12 × £2.50 = £30.00
£52.00 + £30.00 = £82.00
9. **H** 7
$\frac{1}{3}$ of the class returned to school.
21 ÷ 3 = 7
10. **E** 40
17 minutes each way = 34 minutes total
$\frac{34}{85} = \frac{4}{10}$ = 40%

Pages 136–139: Section 3
1. **C** School
The first stop on the 15:15 timetable is the School.
2. **E** High Street
The last stop on the timetable is the High Street.
3. **D** Playground
The bus leaves the Train Station at 14:47 and gets to the Playground at 15:14, a difference of 27 minutes.
4. **E** High Street
The bus stops at the Library at 14:54 and at the School at 15:20, a difference of 26 minutes.
5. **A** Train Station
6. **B** Library
It takes 4 minutes to go from the Train Station to the Library.
7. **C** School
The bus leaves the Train Station at 13:47 and gets to the School at 14:00, a difference of 13 minutes.

8. **E**   High Street
    The bus stops at the Library at 13:52
    and the High Street at 14:13, a
    difference of 21 minutes.
9. **C**   School
10. **D**   Playground
    The journey takes 12 minutes between
    the School and the Playground.
11. **A**   Section A
    A tetrahedron has 4 faces and 6 edges.
12. **E**   Section E
    A cone does not have straight edges.
13. **B**   Section B
    A cuboid has 6 faces and 12 edges.
14. **C**   Section C
    A square-based pyramid has 5 faces
    and 8 edges.
15. **E**   Section E
    A cylinder does not have straight edges.
16. **C**   Section C
    A triangular prism has 5 faces and 9
    edges.
17. **D**   Section D
    A pentagonal prism has 7 faces and 15
    edges.
18. **B**   Section B
    A hexagonal prism has 8 faces and 18
    edges.
19. **E**   Section E
    A sphere does not have straight edges.
20. **B**   Section B
    A cube has 6 faces and 12 edges.
21. **A**   Year 2
    12 children in Year 2 said lollies and 24
    children in Year 4 said lollies, a ratio of
    $1:2$.
22. **B**   Year 3
    9 children in Year 3 said lollies and 18
    children in Year 6 said lollies, a ratio of
    $1:2$.
23. **E**   Year 6
    18 children in Year 6 said lollies.
24. **D**   Year 5
    6 children in Year 5 said lollies.
25. **B**   Year 3
    10 children in Year 3 said chocolates
    and 15 children in Year 2 said
    chocolates.
    $\frac{10}{15} = \frac{2}{3}$
26. **C**   Year 4
    16 children in Year 4 said chocolates
    and 24 children in Year 5 said
    chocolates.
    $\frac{16}{24} = \frac{2}{3}$
27. **C**   Year 4
    16 children in Year 4 said chocolates
    and 8 in Year 6 said chocolates, a ratio
    of $2:1$.
28. **D**   Year 5
    24 children in Year 5 said chocolates
    and 8 in Year 6 said chocolates, a ratio
    of $3:1$.
29. **B**   Year 3
    9 children said lollies and 10 said
    chocolates, a ratio of $9:10$.
30. **D**   Year 5
    6 children said lollies and 24 said
    chocolates, a ratio of $6:24$ or $1:4$.

THIS PAGE HAS DELIBERATELY BEEN LEFT BLANK

Progress Charts

Track your progress by shading in your score at each attempt.

Assessment Papers

	Score	Date:	Attempt 1	Paper 1: Section 1
/38	Score	Date:	Attempt 2	
/19	Score	Date:	Attempt 1	Paper 1: Section 2
/19	Score	Date:	Attempt 2	
/20	Score	Date:	Attempt 1	Paper 1: Section 3
/20	Score	Date:	Attempt 2	
/29	Score	Date:	Attempt 1	Paper 2: Section 1
/29	Score	Date:	Attempt 2	
/30	Score	Date:	Attempt 1	Paper 2: Section 2
/30	Score	Date:	Attempt 2	
/11	Score	Date:	Attempt 1	Paper 2: Section 3
/11	Score	Date:	Attempt 2	
/27	Score	Date:	Attempt 1	Paper 3: Section 1
/27	Score	Date:	Attempt 2	
/10	Score	Date:	Attempt 1	Paper 3: Section 2
/10	Score	Date:	Attempt 2	
/30	Score	Date:	Attempt 1	Paper 3: Section 3
/30	Score	Date:	Attempt 2	

Practice Tests

	Score	Date:	Attempt 1	Practice Test 1: Numeracy
/54	Score	Date:	Attempt 2	
/53	Score	Date:	Attempt 1	Practice Test 2: Numeracy
/53	Score	Date:	Attempt 2	
/30	Score	Date:	Attempt 1	Practice Test 3: Problem Solving
/30	Score	Date:	Attempt 2	
/30	Score	Date:	Attempt 1	Practice Test 4: Problem Solving
/30	Score	Date:	Attempt 2	
/25	Score	Date:	Attempt 1	Practice Test 5: Problem Solving
/25	Score	Date:	Attempt 2	
/25	Score	Date:	Attempt 1	Practice Test 6: Problem Solving
/25	Score	Date:	Attempt 2	
/30	Score	Date:	Attempt 1	Practice Test 7: Cloze
/30	Score	Date:	Attempt 2	
/30	Score	Date:	Attempt 1	Practice Test 8: Cloze
/30	Score	Date:	Attempt 2	

Practice Test 1: Numeracy

Example i		Example ii	
0	0	0	0
1	1	1	1
2	2	2	2
3	3	3	3
4	4	4	4
5	5	5	5
6	6	6	6
7	7	7	7
8	8	8	8
9	9	9	9

1	2	3	4	5	6
0 0	0 0	0 0	0 0	0 0	0 0
1 1	1 1	1 1	1 1	1 1	1 1
2 2	2 2	2 2	2 2	2 2	2 2
3 3	3 3	3 3	3 3	3 3	3 3
4 4	4 4	4 4	4 4	4 4	4 4
5 5	5 5	5 5	5 5	5 5	5 5
6 6	6 6	6 6	6 6	6 6	6 6
7 7	7 7	7 7	7 7	7 7	7 7
8 8	8 8	8 8	8 8	8 8	8 8
9 9	9 9	9 9	9 9	9 9	9 9

7	8	9	10	11	12	13	14
0 0	0 0	0 0	0 0	0 0	0 0	0 0	0 0
1 1	1 1	1 1	1 1	1 1	1 1	1 1	1 1
2 2	2 2	2 2	2 2	2 2	2 2	2 2	2 2
3 3	3 3	3 3	3 3	3 3	3 3	3 3	3 3
4 4	4 4	4 4	4 4	4 4	4 4	4 4	4 4
5 5	5 5	5 5	5 5	5 5	5 5	5 5	5 5
6 6	6 6	6 6	6 6	6 6	6 6	6 6	6 6
7 7	7 7	7 7	7 7	7 7	7 7	7 7	7 7
8 8	8 8	8 8	8 8	8 8	8 8	8 8	8 8
9 9	9 9	9 9	9 9	9 9	9 9	9 9	9 9

15	16	17	18	19	20	21	22
0 0	0 0	0 0	0 0	0 0	0 0	0 0	0 0
1 1	1 1	1 1	1 1	1 1	1 1	1 1	1 1
2 2	2 2	2 2	2 2	2 2	2 2	2 2	2 2
3 3	3 3	3 3	3 3	3 3	3 3	3 3	3 3
4 4	4 4	4 4	4 4	4 4	4 4	4 4	4 4
5 5	5 5	5 5	5 5	5 5	5 5	5 5	5 5
6 6	6 6	6 6	6 6	6 6	6 6	6 6	6 6
7 7	7 7	7 7	7 7	7 7	7 7	7 7	7 7
8 8	8 8	8 8	8 8	8 8	8 8	8 8	8 8
9 9	9 9	9 9	9 9	9 9	9 9	9 9	9 9

23	24	25	26	27	28	29	30
0 0	0 0	0 0	0 0	0 0	0 0	0 0	0 0
1 1	1 1	1 1	1 1	1 1	1 1	1 1	1 1
2 2	2 2	2 2	2 2	2 2	2 2	2 2	2 2
3 3	3 3	3 3	3 3	3 3	3 3	3 3	3 3
4 4	4 4	4 4	4 4	4 4	4 4	4 4	4 4
5 5	5 5	5 5	5 5	5 5	5 5	5 5	5 5
6 6	6 6	6 6	6 6	6 6	6 6	6 6	6 6
7 7	7 7	7 7	7 7	7 7	7 7	7 7	7 7
8 8	8 8	8 8	8 8	8 8	8 8	8 8	8 8
9 9	9 9	9 9	9 9	9 9	9 9	9 9	9 9

Practice Test 1: Numeracy

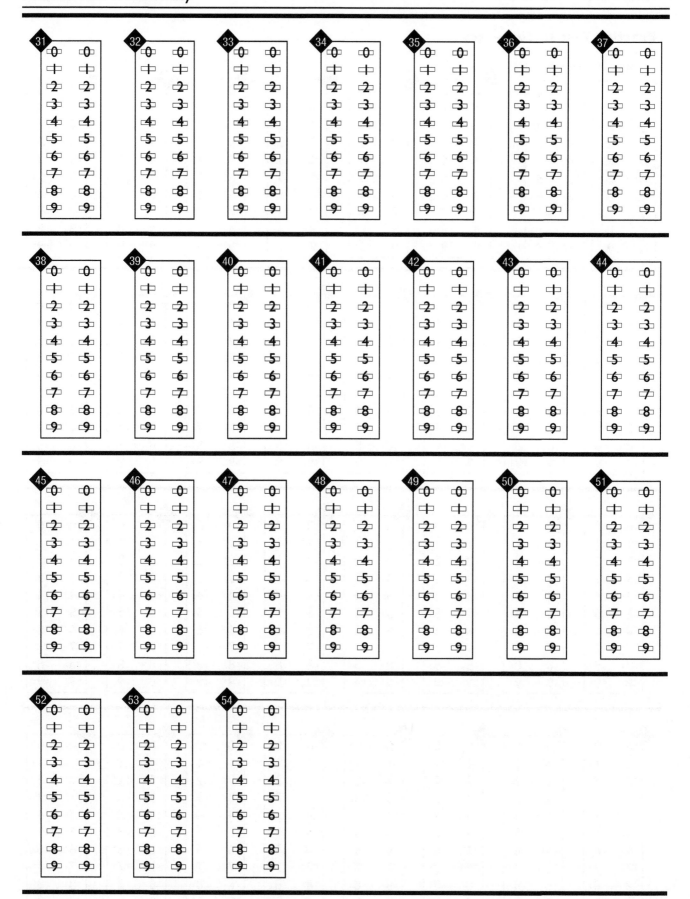

Practice Test 2: Numeracy

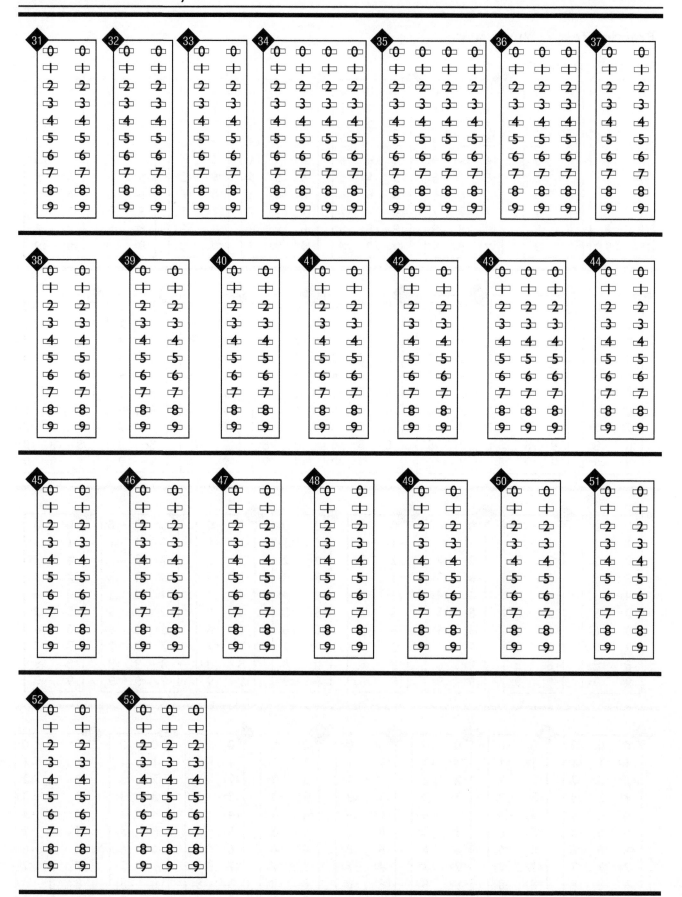

Practice Test 3: Problem Solving

Example i

   A   B   **C**   D   E

Example ii

   A   B   C   D   E

#	A	B	C	D	E
1	A	B	C	D	E
2	A	B	C	D	E
3	A	B	C	D	E
4	A	B	C	D	E
5	A	B	C	D	E
6	A	B	C	D	E
7	A	B	C	D	E
8	A	B	C	D	E
9	A	B	C	D	E
10	A	B	C	D	E
11	A	B	C	D	E
12	A	B	C	D	E
13	A	B	C	D	E
14	A	B	C	D	E
15	A	B	C	D	E
16	A	B	C	D	E
17	A	B	C	D	E
18	A	B	C	D	E
19	A	B	C	D	E
20	A	B	C	D	E
21	A	B	C	D	E
22	A	B	C	D	E
23	A	B	C	D	E
24	A	B	C	D	E
25	A	B	C	D	E
26	A	B	C	D	E
27	A	B	C	D	E
28	A	B	C	D	E
29	A	B	C	D	E
30	A	B	C	D	E

Practice Test 4: Problem Solving

Example i

   A   B   **C**   D   E

Example ii

   A   B   C   D   E

#	A	B	C	D	E
1	A	B	C	D	E
2	A	B	C	D	E
3	A	B	C	D	E
4	A	B	C	D	E
5	A	B	C	D	E
6	A	B	C	D	E
7	A	B	C	D	E
8	A	B	C	D	E
9	A	B	C	D	E
10	A	B	C	D	E
11	A	B	C	D	E
12	A	B	C	D	E
13	A	B	C	D	E
14	A	B	C	D	E
15	A	B	C	D	E
16	A	B	C	D	E
17	A	B	C	D	E
18	A	B	C	D	E
19	A	B	C	D	E
20	A	B	C	D	E
21	A	B	C	D	E
22	A	B	C	D	E
23	A	B	C	D	E
24	A	B	C	D	E
25	A	B	C	D	E
26	A	B	C	D	E
27	A	B	C	D	E
28	A	B	C	D	E
29	A	B	C	D	E
30	A	B	C	D	E

Practice Test 5: Problem Solving

Example i

   A B **C** D E F G H I J

Example ii

   A B C D E F G H I J

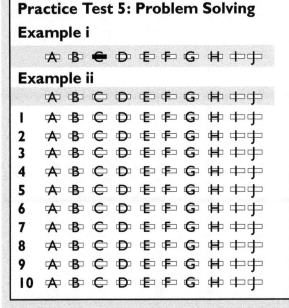

#	A	B	C	D	E	F	G	H	I	J
1	A	B	C	D	E	F	G	H	I	J
2	A	B	C	D	E	F	G	H	I	J
3	A	B	C	D	E	F	G	H	I	J
4	A	B	C	D	E	F	G	H	I	J
5	A	B	C	D	E	F	G	H	I	J
6	A	B	C	D	E	F	G	H	I	J
7	A	B	C	D	E	F	G	H	I	J
8	A	B	C	D	E	F	G	H	I	J
9	A	B	C	D	E	F	G	H	I	J
10	A	B	C	D	E	F	G	H	I	J

#	A	B	C	D	E	F	G	H	I	J	K	L	M	N	O
11	A	B	C	D	E	F	G	H	I	J	K	L	M	N	O
12	A	B	C	D	E	F	G	H	I	J	K	L	M	N	O
13	A	B	C	D	E	F	G	H	I	J	K	L	M	N	O
14	A	B	C	D	E	F	G	H	I	J	K	L	M	N	O
15	A	B	C	D	E	F	G	H	I	J	K	L	M	N	O
16	A	B	C	D	E	F	G	H	I	J	K	L	M	N	O
17	A	B	C	D	E	F	G	H	I	J	K	L	M	N	O
18	A	B	C	D	E	F	G	H	I	J	K	L	M	N	O
19	A	B	C	D	E	F	G	H	I	J	K	L	M	N	O
20	A	B	C	D	E	F	G	H	I	J	K	L	M	N	O
21	A	B	C	D	E	F	G	H	I	J	K	L	M	N	O
22	A	B	C	D	E	F	G	H	I	J	K	L	M	N	O
23	A	B	C	D	E	F	G	H	I	J	K	L	M	N	O
24	A	B	C	D	E	F	G	H	I	J	K	L	M	N	O
25	A	B	C	D	E	F	G	H	I	J	K	L	M	N	O

Practice Test 6: Problem Solving

Example i

Ⓐ Ⓑ ⬤ Ⓓ Ⓔ Ⓕ Ⓖ Ⓗ Ⓘ Ⓙ

Example ii

Ⓐ Ⓑ Ⓒ Ⓓ Ⓔ Ⓕ Ⓖ Ⓗ Ⓘ Ⓙ

1 Ⓐ Ⓑ Ⓒ Ⓓ Ⓔ Ⓕ Ⓖ Ⓗ Ⓘ Ⓙ
2 Ⓐ Ⓑ Ⓒ Ⓓ Ⓔ Ⓕ Ⓖ Ⓗ Ⓘ Ⓙ
3 Ⓐ Ⓑ Ⓒ Ⓓ Ⓔ Ⓕ Ⓖ Ⓗ Ⓘ Ⓙ
4 Ⓐ Ⓑ Ⓒ Ⓓ Ⓔ Ⓕ Ⓖ Ⓗ Ⓘ Ⓙ
5 Ⓐ Ⓑ Ⓒ Ⓓ Ⓔ Ⓕ Ⓖ Ⓗ Ⓘ Ⓙ
6 Ⓐ Ⓑ Ⓒ Ⓓ Ⓔ Ⓕ Ⓖ Ⓗ Ⓘ Ⓙ
7 Ⓐ Ⓑ Ⓒ Ⓓ Ⓔ Ⓕ Ⓖ Ⓗ Ⓘ Ⓙ
8 Ⓐ Ⓑ Ⓒ Ⓓ Ⓔ Ⓕ Ⓖ Ⓗ Ⓘ Ⓙ
9 Ⓐ Ⓑ Ⓒ Ⓓ Ⓔ Ⓕ Ⓖ Ⓗ Ⓘ Ⓙ
10 Ⓐ Ⓑ Ⓒ Ⓓ Ⓔ Ⓕ Ⓖ Ⓗ Ⓘ Ⓙ

11 Ⓐ Ⓑ Ⓒ Ⓓ Ⓔ Ⓕ Ⓖ Ⓗ Ⓘ Ⓙ Ⓚ Ⓛ Ⓜ Ⓝ Ⓞ
12 Ⓐ Ⓑ Ⓒ Ⓓ Ⓔ Ⓕ Ⓖ Ⓗ Ⓘ Ⓙ Ⓚ Ⓛ Ⓜ Ⓝ Ⓞ
13 Ⓐ Ⓑ Ⓒ Ⓓ Ⓔ Ⓕ Ⓖ Ⓗ Ⓘ Ⓙ Ⓚ Ⓛ Ⓜ Ⓝ Ⓞ
14 Ⓐ Ⓑ Ⓒ Ⓓ Ⓔ Ⓕ Ⓖ Ⓗ Ⓘ Ⓙ Ⓚ Ⓛ Ⓜ Ⓝ Ⓞ
15 Ⓐ Ⓑ Ⓒ Ⓓ Ⓔ Ⓕ Ⓖ Ⓗ Ⓘ Ⓙ Ⓚ Ⓛ Ⓜ Ⓝ Ⓞ
16 Ⓐ Ⓑ Ⓒ Ⓓ Ⓔ Ⓕ Ⓖ Ⓗ Ⓘ Ⓙ Ⓚ Ⓛ Ⓜ Ⓝ Ⓞ
17 Ⓐ Ⓑ Ⓒ Ⓓ Ⓔ Ⓕ Ⓖ Ⓗ Ⓘ Ⓙ Ⓚ Ⓛ Ⓜ Ⓝ Ⓞ
18 Ⓐ Ⓑ Ⓒ Ⓓ Ⓔ Ⓕ Ⓖ Ⓗ Ⓘ Ⓙ Ⓚ Ⓛ Ⓜ Ⓝ Ⓞ
19 Ⓐ Ⓑ Ⓒ Ⓓ Ⓔ Ⓕ Ⓖ Ⓗ Ⓘ Ⓙ Ⓚ Ⓛ Ⓜ Ⓝ Ⓞ
20 Ⓐ Ⓑ Ⓒ Ⓓ Ⓔ Ⓕ Ⓖ Ⓗ Ⓘ Ⓙ Ⓚ Ⓛ Ⓜ Ⓝ Ⓞ
21 Ⓐ Ⓑ Ⓒ Ⓓ Ⓔ Ⓕ Ⓖ Ⓗ Ⓘ Ⓙ Ⓚ Ⓛ Ⓜ Ⓝ Ⓞ
22 Ⓐ Ⓑ Ⓒ Ⓓ Ⓔ Ⓕ Ⓖ Ⓗ Ⓘ Ⓙ Ⓚ Ⓛ Ⓜ Ⓝ Ⓞ
23 Ⓐ Ⓑ Ⓒ Ⓓ Ⓔ Ⓕ Ⓖ Ⓗ Ⓘ Ⓙ Ⓚ Ⓛ Ⓜ Ⓝ Ⓞ
24 Ⓐ Ⓑ Ⓒ Ⓓ Ⓔ Ⓕ Ⓖ Ⓗ Ⓘ Ⓙ Ⓚ Ⓛ Ⓜ Ⓝ Ⓞ
25 Ⓐ Ⓑ Ⓒ Ⓓ Ⓔ Ⓕ Ⓖ Ⓗ Ⓘ Ⓙ Ⓚ Ⓛ Ⓜ Ⓝ Ⓞ

Practice Test 7: Cloze

Example i

Ⓐ Ⓑ ⬤ Ⓓ Ⓔ

Example ii

Ⓐ Ⓑ Ⓒ Ⓓ Ⓔ

1 Ⓐ Ⓑ Ⓒ Ⓓ Ⓔ
2 Ⓐ Ⓑ Ⓒ Ⓓ Ⓔ
3 Ⓐ Ⓑ Ⓒ Ⓓ Ⓔ
4 Ⓐ Ⓑ Ⓒ Ⓓ Ⓔ
5 Ⓐ Ⓑ Ⓒ Ⓓ Ⓔ
6 Ⓐ Ⓑ Ⓒ Ⓓ Ⓔ
7 Ⓐ Ⓑ Ⓒ Ⓓ Ⓔ
8 Ⓐ Ⓑ Ⓒ Ⓓ Ⓔ
9 Ⓐ Ⓑ Ⓒ Ⓓ Ⓔ
10 Ⓐ Ⓑ Ⓒ Ⓓ Ⓔ
11 Ⓐ Ⓑ Ⓒ Ⓓ Ⓔ
12 Ⓐ Ⓑ Ⓒ Ⓓ Ⓔ
13 Ⓐ Ⓑ Ⓒ Ⓓ Ⓔ
14 Ⓐ Ⓑ Ⓒ Ⓓ Ⓔ
15 Ⓐ Ⓑ Ⓒ Ⓓ Ⓔ
16 Ⓐ Ⓑ Ⓒ Ⓓ Ⓔ
17 Ⓐ Ⓑ Ⓒ Ⓓ Ⓔ
18 Ⓐ Ⓑ Ⓒ Ⓓ Ⓔ
19 Ⓐ Ⓑ Ⓒ Ⓓ Ⓔ
20 Ⓐ Ⓑ Ⓒ Ⓓ Ⓔ
21 Ⓐ Ⓑ Ⓒ Ⓓ Ⓔ
22 Ⓐ Ⓑ Ⓒ Ⓓ Ⓔ
23 Ⓐ Ⓑ Ⓒ Ⓓ Ⓔ
24 Ⓐ Ⓑ Ⓒ Ⓓ Ⓔ
25 Ⓐ Ⓑ Ⓒ Ⓓ Ⓔ
26 Ⓐ Ⓑ Ⓒ Ⓓ Ⓔ
27 Ⓐ Ⓑ Ⓒ Ⓓ Ⓔ
28 Ⓐ Ⓑ Ⓒ Ⓓ Ⓔ
29 Ⓐ Ⓑ Ⓒ Ⓓ Ⓔ
30 Ⓐ Ⓑ Ⓒ Ⓓ Ⓔ

Practice Test 8: Cloze

Example i

Ⓐ Ⓑ ⬤ Ⓓ Ⓔ

Example ii

Ⓐ Ⓑ Ⓒ Ⓓ Ⓔ

1 Ⓐ Ⓑ Ⓒ Ⓓ Ⓔ
2 Ⓐ Ⓑ Ⓒ Ⓓ Ⓔ
3 Ⓐ Ⓑ Ⓒ Ⓓ Ⓔ
4 Ⓐ Ⓑ Ⓒ Ⓓ Ⓔ
5 Ⓐ Ⓑ Ⓒ Ⓓ Ⓔ
6 Ⓐ Ⓑ Ⓒ Ⓓ Ⓔ
7 Ⓐ Ⓑ Ⓒ Ⓓ Ⓔ
8 Ⓐ Ⓑ Ⓒ Ⓓ Ⓔ
9 Ⓐ Ⓑ Ⓒ Ⓓ Ⓔ
10 Ⓐ Ⓑ Ⓒ Ⓓ Ⓔ
11 Ⓐ Ⓑ Ⓒ Ⓓ Ⓔ
12 Ⓐ Ⓑ Ⓒ Ⓓ Ⓔ
13 Ⓐ Ⓑ Ⓒ Ⓓ Ⓔ
14 Ⓐ Ⓑ Ⓒ Ⓓ Ⓔ
15 Ⓐ Ⓑ Ⓒ Ⓓ Ⓔ
16 Ⓐ Ⓑ Ⓒ Ⓓ Ⓔ
17 Ⓐ Ⓑ Ⓒ Ⓓ Ⓔ
18 Ⓐ Ⓑ Ⓒ Ⓓ Ⓔ
19 Ⓐ Ⓑ Ⓒ Ⓓ Ⓔ
20 Ⓐ Ⓑ Ⓒ Ⓓ Ⓔ
21 Ⓐ Ⓑ Ⓒ Ⓓ Ⓔ
22 Ⓐ Ⓑ Ⓒ Ⓓ Ⓔ
23 Ⓐ Ⓑ Ⓒ Ⓓ Ⓔ
24 Ⓐ Ⓑ Ⓒ Ⓓ Ⓔ
25 Ⓐ Ⓑ Ⓒ Ⓓ Ⓔ
26 Ⓐ Ⓑ Ⓒ Ⓓ Ⓔ
27 Ⓐ Ⓑ Ⓒ Ⓓ Ⓔ
28 Ⓐ Ⓑ Ⓒ Ⓓ Ⓔ
29 Ⓐ Ⓑ Ⓒ Ⓓ Ⓔ
30 Ⓐ Ⓑ Ⓒ Ⓓ Ⓔ

Pupil's Full Name:

Instructions:
Mark the boxes correctly like this ✈

Please sign your name here:

Section 1

Example i	Example ii

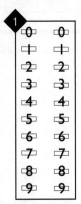
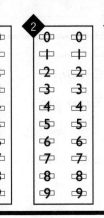
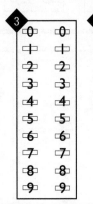

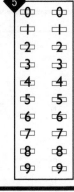
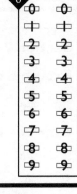

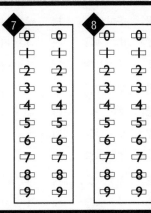
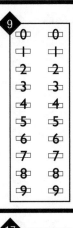
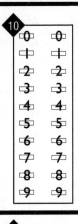
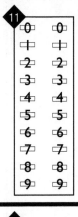
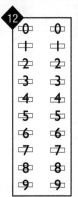

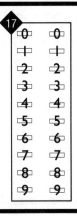
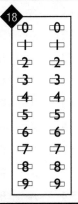
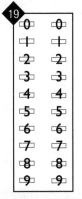
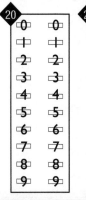

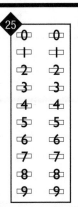
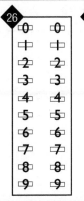

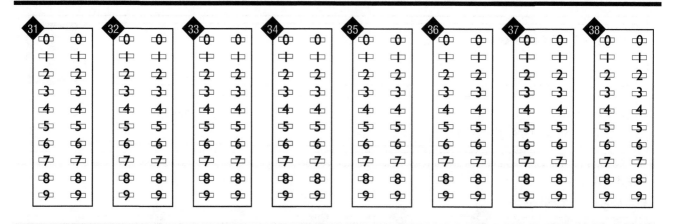

Section 2

Example i

A ⬥   B   C   D   E

Example ii

A   B   C   D   E

1	A	B	C	D	E
2	A	B	C	D	E
3	A	B	C	D	E
4	A	B	C	D	E
5	A	B	C	D	E
6	A	B	C	D	E
7	A	B	C	D	E
8	A	B	C	D	E
9	A	B	C	D	E
10	A	B	C	D	E
11	A	B	C	D	E
12	A	B	C	D	E
13	A	B	C	D	E
14	A	B	C	D	E
15	A	B	C	D	E
16	A	B	C	D	E
17	A	B	C	D	E
18	A	B	C	D	E
19	A	B	C	D	E

Section 3

Example i

A ⬥   B   C   D   E   F   G   H   I   J

Example ii

A   B   C   D   E   F   G   H   I   J

1	A	B	C	D	E	F	G	H	I	J
2	A	B	C	D	E	F	G	H	I	J
3	A	B	C	D	E	F	G	H	I	J
4	A	B	C	D	E	F	G	H	I	J
5	A	B	C	D	E	F	G	H	I	J
6	A	B	C	D	E	F	G	H	I	J
7	A	B	C	D	E	F	G	H	I	J
8	A	B	C	D	E	F	G	H	I	J
9	A	B	C	D	E	F	G	H	I	J
10	A	B	C	D	E	F	G	H	I	J
11	A	B	C	D	E	F	G	H	I	J
12	A	B	C	D	E	F	G	H	I	J
13	A	B	C	D	E	F	G	H	I	J
14	A	B	C	D	E	F	G	H	I	J
15	A	B	C	D	E	F	G	H	I	J
16	A	B	C	D	E	F	G	H	I	J
17	A	B	C	D	E	F	G	H	I	J
18	A	B	C	D	E	F	G	H	I	J
19	A	B	C	D	E	F	G	H	I	J
20	A	B	C	D	E	F	G	H	I	J

Pupil's Full Name:

2

Instructions:
Mark the boxes correctly like this ✦

Please sign your name here:

Section 1

Example i

	A	B	C	D	✦

Example ii

	A	B	C	D	E

	A	B	C	D	E
1	A	B	C	D	E
2	A	B	C	D	E
3	A	B	C	D	E
4	A	B	C	D	E
5	A	B	C	D	E
6	A	B	C	D	E
7	A	B	C	D	E
8	A	B	C	D	E
9	A	B	C	D	E
10	A	B	C	D	E
11	A	B	C	D	E
12	A	B	C	D	E
13	A	B	C	D	E
14	A	B	C	D	E
15	A	B	C	D	E
16	A	B	C	D	E
17	A	B	C	D	E
18	A	B	C	D	E
19	A	B	C	D	E
20	A	B	C	D	E
21	A	B	C	D	E
22	A	B	C	D	E
23	A	B	C	D	E
24	A	B	C	D	E
25	A	B	C	D	E
26	A	B	C	D	E
27	A	B	C	D	E
28	A	B	C	D	E
29	A	B	C	D	E

Section 2

Example i

	A	✦	C	D	E

Example ii

	A	B	C	D	E

	A	B	C	D	E
1	A	B	C	D	E
2	A	B	C	D	E
3	A	B	C	D	E
4	A	B	C	D	E
5	A	B	C	D	E
6	A	B	C	D	E
7	A	B	C	D	E
8	A	B	C	D	E
9	A	B	C	D	E
10	A	B	C	D	E
11	A	B	C	D	E
12	A	B	C	D	E
13	A	B	C	D	E
14	A	B	C	D	E
15	A	B	C	D	E
16	A	B	C	D	E
17	A	B	C	D	E
18	A	B	C	D	E
19	A	B	C	D	E
20	A	B	C	D	E
21	A	B	C	D	E
22	A	B	C	D	E
23	A	B	C	D	E
24	A	B	C	D	E
25	A	B	C	D	E
26	A	B	C	D	E
27	A	B	C	D	E
28	A	B	C	D	E
29	A	B	C	D	E
30	A	B	C	D	E

Section 3

Example i

| A | B | C | D | E | F | G | H | I | J |

Example ii

| A | B | C | D | E | F | G | H | I | J |

	A	B	C	D	E	F	G	H	I	J
1	A	B	C	D	E	F	G	H	I	J
2	A	B	C	D	E	F	G	H	I	J
3	A	B	C	D	E	F	G	H	I	J
4	A	B	C	D	E	F	G	H	I	J
5	A	B	C	D	E	F	G	H	I	J
6	A	B	C	D	E	F	G	H	I	J
7	A	B	C	D	E	F	G	H	I	J
8	A	B	C	D	E	F	G	H	I	J
9	A	B	C	D	E	F	G	H	I	J
10	A	B	C	D	E	F	G	H	I	J
11	A	B	C	D	E	F	G	H	I	J

Pupil's Full Name:

3

Instructions:
Mark the boxes correctly like this ★

Please sign your name here:

Section 1

Example i

	Ⓐ	Ⓑ	Ⓒ	Ⓓ	★

Example ii

	Ⓐ	Ⓑ	Ⓒ	Ⓓ	Ⓔ
1	Ⓐ	Ⓑ	Ⓒ	Ⓓ	Ⓔ
2	Ⓐ	Ⓑ	Ⓒ	Ⓓ	Ⓔ
3	Ⓐ	Ⓑ	Ⓒ	Ⓓ	Ⓔ
4	Ⓐ	Ⓑ	Ⓒ	Ⓓ	Ⓔ
5	Ⓐ	Ⓑ	Ⓒ	Ⓓ	Ⓔ
6	Ⓐ	Ⓑ	Ⓒ	Ⓓ	Ⓔ
7	Ⓐ	Ⓑ	Ⓒ	Ⓓ	Ⓔ
8	Ⓐ	Ⓑ	Ⓒ	Ⓓ	Ⓔ
9	Ⓐ	Ⓑ	Ⓒ	Ⓓ	Ⓔ
10	Ⓐ	Ⓑ	Ⓒ	Ⓓ	Ⓔ
11	Ⓐ	Ⓑ	Ⓒ	Ⓓ	Ⓔ
12	Ⓐ	Ⓑ	Ⓒ	Ⓓ	Ⓔ
13	Ⓐ	Ⓑ	Ⓒ	Ⓓ	Ⓔ
14	Ⓐ	Ⓑ	Ⓒ	Ⓓ	Ⓔ
15	Ⓐ	Ⓑ	Ⓒ	Ⓓ	Ⓔ
16	Ⓐ	Ⓑ	Ⓒ	Ⓓ	Ⓔ
17	Ⓐ	Ⓑ	Ⓒ	Ⓓ	Ⓔ
18	Ⓐ	Ⓑ	Ⓒ	Ⓓ	Ⓔ
19	Ⓐ	Ⓑ	Ⓒ	Ⓓ	Ⓔ
20	Ⓐ	Ⓑ	Ⓒ	Ⓓ	Ⓔ
21	Ⓐ	Ⓑ	Ⓒ	Ⓓ	Ⓔ
22	Ⓐ	Ⓑ	Ⓒ	Ⓓ	Ⓔ
23	Ⓐ	Ⓑ	Ⓒ	Ⓓ	Ⓔ
24	Ⓐ	Ⓑ	Ⓒ	Ⓓ	Ⓔ
25	Ⓐ	Ⓑ	Ⓒ	Ⓓ	Ⓔ
26	Ⓐ	Ⓑ	Ⓒ	Ⓓ	Ⓔ
27	Ⓐ	Ⓑ	Ⓒ	Ⓓ	Ⓔ

Section 2

Example i

	★	Ⓑ	Ⓒ	Ⓓ	Ⓔ	Ⓕ	Ⓖ	Ⓗ	Ⓘ	Ⓙ

Example ii

	Ⓐ	Ⓑ	Ⓒ	Ⓓ	Ⓔ	Ⓕ	Ⓖ	Ⓗ	Ⓘ	Ⓙ
1	Ⓐ	Ⓑ	Ⓒ	Ⓓ	Ⓔ	Ⓕ	Ⓖ	Ⓗ	Ⓘ	Ⓙ
2	Ⓐ	Ⓑ	Ⓒ	Ⓓ	Ⓔ	Ⓕ	Ⓖ	Ⓗ	Ⓘ	Ⓙ
3	Ⓐ	Ⓑ	Ⓒ	Ⓓ	Ⓔ	Ⓕ	Ⓖ	Ⓗ	Ⓘ	Ⓙ
4	Ⓐ	Ⓑ	Ⓒ	Ⓓ	Ⓔ	Ⓕ	Ⓖ	Ⓗ	Ⓘ	Ⓙ
5	Ⓐ	Ⓑ	Ⓒ	Ⓓ	Ⓔ	Ⓕ	Ⓖ	Ⓗ	Ⓘ	Ⓙ
6	Ⓐ	Ⓑ	Ⓒ	Ⓓ	Ⓔ	Ⓕ	Ⓖ	Ⓗ	Ⓘ	Ⓙ
7	Ⓐ	Ⓑ	Ⓒ	Ⓓ	Ⓔ	Ⓕ	Ⓖ	Ⓗ	Ⓘ	Ⓙ
8	Ⓐ	Ⓑ	Ⓒ	Ⓓ	Ⓔ	Ⓕ	Ⓖ	Ⓗ	Ⓘ	Ⓙ
9	Ⓐ	Ⓑ	Ⓒ	Ⓓ	Ⓔ	Ⓕ	Ⓖ	Ⓗ	Ⓘ	Ⓙ
10	Ⓐ	Ⓑ	Ⓒ	Ⓓ	Ⓔ	Ⓕ	Ⓖ	Ⓗ	Ⓘ	Ⓙ

Section 3

Example i

	A	B	C	D	E

Example ii

	A	B	C	D	E
1	A	B	C	D	E
2	A	B	C	D	E
3	A	B	C	D	E
4	A	B	C	D	E
5	A	B	C	D	E
6	A	B	C	D	E
7	A	B	C	D	E
8	A	B	C	D	E
9	A	B	C	D	E
10	A	B	C	D	E
11	A	B	C	D	E
12	A	B	C	D	E
13	A	B	C	D	E
14	A	B	C	D	E
15	A	B	C	D	E
16	A	B	C	D	E
17	A	B	C	D	E
18	A	B	C	D	E
19	A	B	C	D	E
20	A	B	C	D	E
21	A	B	C	D	E
22	A	B	C	D	E
23	A	B	C	D	E
24	A	B	C	D	E
25	A	B	C	D	E
26	A	B	C	D	E
27	A	B	C	D	E
28	A	B	C	D	E
29	A	B	C	D	E
30	A	B	C	D	E